BOOK 2: RISE OF THE PARENT

SAVING THE WORLD
ONE BOOB AT A TIME

Shona Reidy

Copyright © 2024 by Shona Reidy

All rights reserved. No part of this publication may be reproduced, distributed, or transmitted in any form or by any means, including photocopying, recording, or other electronic or mechanical methods, without the prior written permission of the publisher, except in the case of brief quotations embodied in critical reviews and certain other noncommercial uses permitted by copyright law.

Book Design by HMDpublishing

ISBN: 978-0-6456805-3-9

Instagram Handle: @savingtheworldoneboobatatime

Disclaimer: This book is based on true events however all names have been changed to protect the identity of all people for personal and legal reasons, the author maintains that any character's resemblance to real, living persons is just a coincidence.

For my babies, you gave me the strength to find myself xxx

CONTENTS

INTRODUCTION................................5

CHAPTER 1.
THE END IS ALWAYS THE BEGINNING. WEANING.........8

CHAPTER 2.
MEETING FRANK.................................21

CHAPTER 3.
THE TRUTH ABOUT FRANK AND ME.................36

CHAPTER 4.
MORE TRUTHS.................................47

CHAPTER 5.
MORE AND MORE.................................63

CHAPTER 6.
ABUSING THE "MOTHER"........................73

CHAPTER 7.
THE BABY ARRIVES.............................86

CHAPTER 8.
THE ANGER ARRIVES............................101

CHAPTER 9.
BOXING DAY...................................116

CHAPTER 10.
*MY SON ARRIVES, ALONG WITH A LOT MORE ABUSE....*129

CHAPTER 11.
THE DARKNESS CONTINUES.......................155

CHAPTER 12.
WHAT HAPPENS WHEN WE BECOME PARENTS?.......175

CHAPTER 13.
MOVE FORWARD - ALWAYS MOVE FORWARD........179

RESOURCES FOR HELP............................182

ABOUT THE AUTHOR..............................184

INTRODUCTION

Once I commenced my journey into becoming a breastfeeding counsellor, I set myself a mission:

"Save the world, one boob at a time."

But what is the mission once we stop breastfeeding?

This became a quandary for me once I weaned my daughter. Who was I meant to be to her now? How did I become a parent? What is the solution for *rising* as a parent?

This book is dedicated to women who can feel that inner-wolf inside them howling to be given permission to listen to the churning in her stomach... to be reassured that anxiety is just your instincts turning on!

That the fear you are feeling is your instincts giving you *permission* to protect your child.

That strength you feel in your stomach when that stranger tries to kiss your baby is your *instincts*, ready to swipe their face in case they try.

This story is the one that appears for you when the days of waiting for them to say "I love you, mummy/daddy" are over; it is one that is found when you discover that you and your child actually have a relationship that is more than just mouth to boob, changing nappies and trying to put to sleep.

This relationship is unlike any interaction with another human being you have ever had before.

It encompasses decisions, responsibility and, most of all, it involves using all of your heart to guide another human being. A human being that you once simply had to pick up, to satisfy all of their emotional needs.

As parent, you have to talk, you have to interact, you have to explain things, even yourself, and most of all, you have to be the best version of you that you can possibly be. Or else they call "bullshit!" on you.

Children sniff a lie a mile away, lean into truth as if it's the only thing that matters, and love, love and more love is what they crave. Not just "I love you" words type of love – real love, in everything life throws at you and everything you throw at life. Love can be found in anger, tears and frustration. Love is not just a cuddle and a kiss; it is also in saying NO and in disciplining the behaviours that can be projections of how that child feels as they are growing.

To be the best parent you can possibly be, you have to step up, and RISE. *Every. Single. Day.*

You make a mistake, you apologise.

You fall down, you get back up again.

You succeed, you celebrate.

You show them how to live it.

You remain present, you pay attention, and you chose them. Chose THEM, by choosing YOU first.

If you are wondering if you are doing it right, if you are feeling guilty and miserable and ashamed at your own sense of self in life, this book is for you.

This book is aimed to show you how to be the best version of yourself – a version that is honest, safe and loving. No matter what situation you have 'found yourself in' once you become a parent, I hope that by writing my own personal journey of rising out of my own situation will inspire you to polish your sword and hold up your shield.

You are in the middle of the battlefield and you are raising the future army. Rise, parent, *RISE!*

Chapter 1

THE END IS ALWAYS THE BEGINNING. WEANING.

Weaning Emily came as much as a surprise to me as it did to her.

One evening, we are having "milky-time" and just as she latches on, I push – more like shove – her off me, hard and fast.

"Surprise!" and I actually have a fleeting thought: *I want to slap her face.*

"Mummy!" Emily stops, startled. She looks at me, tears forming in her eyes. "What's wrong? Why did you push me away?"

Tears form in my own eyes. I am shocked at myself and quickly bring her to back to my breast. I tell her I made a mistake and was just being silly and blah-blah-blah, scramble-scramble-scramble. As she latches on, the feeling of someone scratching their fingernails down a chalkboard screeches in my ears. I feel a long painful nerve run from my neck all the way down to my waist.

I am two years into being a National Helpline Breastfeeding Counsellor (Emily is a month away from turning three) and I know instantly what this is: "Breastfeeding Aversion".

I am shocked. Really. Truly. *Gobsmacked.*

"Not me," I think. "*No way!*" I gasp internally. I cannot in a million years believe that I, Elizabeth Ann, the mummy who gets her boobs out in public, breastfed her daughter on a plane sort-of-mum, can honestly have breastfeeding AVERSION?

"It doesn't make sense!" I ruminate throughout that feed, struggling with the nerves jangling up and down my spine, feeling guilty for having pushed Emily – no, it was a shove; I am pretty sure I just *shoved* my daughter off my boob – and feeling shocked that I even thought about slapping her – *did I really just think that?* I am shocked out of my mind. *What on earth is this feeling?* – and saddened that I have to be the one to end this relationship. Because even though I know it's not how I thought our breastfeeding relationship would end, I know that it's important I put in a plan of weaning ASAP.

You see, breast-feeding is a relationship, just like any other, and when one person in that relationship isn't interested any more, or is hormonally 'averted' from wanting to participate, then it is *toxic* for the other party for you to both continue. Breast-feeding through aversion is negative and emotionally taxing for the mum. It's also feeding your child 'negative' breastmilk energy. The energy exchange is toxic and this can affect the relationship 'outside' of breastfeed too. A mother can start to resent her child wanting comfort at the breast, and then this can transpire to resenting her child wanting comfort 'just in case they want the breast'. The psychological link can transfer from breast to life and, although repair can be done, it is best to understand this now before you persist because you are determined that "breast is best".

That's right, you heard it here: breast is *NOT ALWAYS* best. Especially with aversion.

There are no ifs or buts. If you get breastfeeding aversion, it is not you – it is the hormones, and it is time to finish breastfeeding. NOW.

I put Emily to sleep. I look at the calendar and start to read up on what I need to do to wean.

"Usually," I start to counsel myself here, trying to push away the fight or flight nervous system from upsetting the good advice I know I have within me, "we recommend you drop the most favourite feed every three to five days until there are no feeds left."

Okay, I *decide instantly, it happens tomorrow.* I cannot imagine the thought of those nerves going up and down my spine for much longer. I shudder again and then put my plan into place.

She's feeding about a million times a day! I have no idea how I'm going to do this, and so I pour myself a glass of wine, roll myself a cigarette, and then cry my eyes out.

I don't tell Frank. He has been wanting me to wean since she was six months old, to see him secretly delighted would push me to the edge…and I'm already dangling over it, so I refrain from imparting how I feel. We are nearly two years since he hit me anyway, so I don't trust him to have my back. (Yes, I am that girl you are yelling at the TV to "Leave him, sister!" I'm still with a guy that hit me, but more on that later. I promise you, it gets worse before it gets better.)

The next morning when she asks for "milky-time" I am worn out from the slightly-too-much wine the night before and I forget to prepare myself for that morning feed.

"Whoops!" She latches on. The jarring sensation of nerves clanging up and down my spine go off like an internal alarm bell.

"FUCK ME!" I say this out loud.

Emily looks up at me, but doesn't spit out the nipple. She smiles, I soften at that smile, I always do, but I'm in a *lot* of emotional pain.

She stops and is satisfied, but I can tell she's watching me and I feel like I'm losing my Magic Power. She's starting to realise I'm a human and that terrifies me.

"Because one day she'll know I'm shit," I admonish myself like I do.

"I'm okay," I answer a question that wasn't asked out loud. "I love you *so* much."

I reassure her and when she's busy playing with toys I go to look at the calendar. It's one month until Emily is three. I like even numbers in life, you know, milestones, etc.

"I breastfed Emily for three years exactly." I say it out loud...but not too loud. I don't want her to hear me, she's so bloody smart. Who knows if she will catch onto me?

I recall in my studies as a counsellor that a cuddle toy is recommended to help her emotionally feel soothed when the milk goes away, so I buy her a

11

really cool and soft teddy bear. I then sit her down after discussing all of this with Frank.

I have brushed over it with him at breakfast. I ensured I didn't smile or frown or cry, but I'm an open book. I know he knows I am defeated and I hate that he is looking happy about it.

Frank is sitting there looking excited. I can tell he feels he may get closer to his daughter. To be fair, she's not real keen on Frank. She just loves her mummy so much. Emily quite often openly tells Frank, "No, I want to be with Mummy." I used to empathise with him, until he started to lash out at me. That's another chapter: don't worry – life always gets way more hectic for Elizabeth Ann!

Frank's job is to help distract Emily during the day if she ever needs "milky-time".

He is all for it, very keen to get her 'off the breast', as he feels the age of three is way too old anyway. Well, Frank's mother does and Frank is completely under the influence of mummy ever since he became a father.

If not for my strong instincts, there's no way I would have ever been able to override his wishes if it wasn't for that newfound strength to honour my child over anyone else.

Those instincts are *strong*!

He is also to help her love her new teddy bear. This, I knew he would agree to wholeheartedly, constantly miffed and just outright pissed off, anything to take his daughter's focus off her mum, he is excited about. (I know, what a supportive husband!)

So, I have my strategy and my weaning chapter begins.

I decide – after much collaboration with my Breastfeeding Counsellor colleagues, trainers and assessors and the text books – to tell her that the 'milk will go when she turns three'. I tell her, "It's just something that 'happens' to mummies when big girls turn three," and, "There is nothing we can do about it."

"Mummy is sad too," I tell her. I recall crying when breaking this news to her, as she immediately burst into tears.

"But look," I say to distract her. "Daddy has a toy to cuddle and you're a big girl now and let's celebrate that!"

Even writing this, I feel a pang of guilt about lying.

It all sounds like such bullshit now, but the alternative was thoughts of slapping her face and I've counselled literally thousands of mothers who have all said the same thing:

"Want to slap, won't do it, but *my goodness!* really wanted to."

I reassure them; it's not them, it's just the aversion. It's not you, it's the hormones.

Bloody, fucking, hormones, eh?

So we start the distraction techniques over the first two weeks and after twelve days we are down to one feed at night. This one will be the hardest to let go.

I have a few nights without the nerve jarring down my spine and wonder if I can possibly continue on just the one feed. However, the next few nights the nerves are back again and I know, without a doubt, I need to wean. I can't stand it.

Third birthday rolls around.

I give Emily her last feed. She cuddles up to me. She is tired after a big day. So am I, in fact. Turning three is hard work for mums as well.

I watch her as she suckles for the last time.

I watch her as she pulls off for the last time.

I cry silently as I gently put my breast away for what I thought would be the last time.

I put my finger in the palm of her left hand and she instinctively grabs hold of it.

I lay staring at her for a long, long time. Remembering when she was just born.

Feeling the marvel of how fast she has grown into a little girl, but when she sleeps looks like that newborn angel again.

Overwhelmed with gratitude that she chose me as her Mummy. Realising how incredible life is as a mother and feeling thankful that I got to not just experience breastfeeding but learn about it for three beautiful years. Marvelling at the turn in my life breastfeeding has taken, from loving it, to learning how to counsel it, to becoming a Group Leader at a local ABA branch, to being on the National Helpline. I am so grateful at what it has shown me and taught me and nurtured me with. I stare at her one last time, give her a kiss on the head, whisper, "Mummy loves you" in her ear – I still do this to both of my children, every single night, hoping that it permeates their dreams and stops any nightmares ruining their slumber – and walk down to the kitchen to pour myself the biggest glass of wine I can possibly find.

In the morning Emily asks me straight away if the milk has gone.

I stop and look at her with sadness and love, so much love. I say, "Yes darling," and she cries.

I sit with her on the couch and we both cry together. (I actually cry whilst writing this and also cry every time I read it. Tears of heart ached and joy.)

I'm nursing a headache from the wine I drank the night before and also allowing the overspill of emotion from her get caught up in my own 'end of chapter' journey.

Oh *FUCK*, I think to myself. *I feel like the shittest mum in the world. What have I done? Why couldn't I just put up with it?*

I then do a quick mental recall of those nerve jars down my spine and I inwardly shudder.

Nope, I'm done, we're done, just stop...

I go and bring out the teddy that we got her to 'comfort her' and she holds onto it gingerly, like she doesn't want to like it, because if she rejects it, the milk might come back.

I know my daughter and I sense this and I reassure her that Mummy is still here, and Mummy isn't ever going away and that she can still do everything else she did with Mummy, but there's just no more milk left.

Emily, who is smarter than me, looks at my chest, looks up and me and then decides on the solution,

"OK, so can I still cuddle the milky then?"

15

I stare at her, not expecting this at all. "What do you mean?"

She replies, "Cuddle it, without having the milk."

I stare again, thinking. *Um, is this allowed? Not in my text books this one.*

"Um," I fumble, stretching the corners of my brain trying to make the 'right' decision here. After all, I can ruin her for life with this one decision can't I?

First-time-mum panic hits me and I scramble for a while with this, umming and ahhhing until eventually I do my quick three step checklist – is it safe, loving and respectful? I can tick off all three, so, why not?

"Well yes of course you can cuddle it," I spit out eventually, "But no drinking it, okay?"

"Okay, Mummy," and she reaches her hand into my dress. I take her hand out, remind her we don't reach down mummy's dress, and I pull out my right breast.

She leans her cheek next to it and places her right hand on the top and her left hand on the bottom of it.

She sits there and watches morning cartoons. I drink my coffee and watch the cartoons too, with a somewhat stunned 'um, nothing-to-see-here' look on my face.

Then the panic sets in. My abusive and controlling husband is going to FUCKING *HATE* this!

I ruminate on all the words. "This is normal, yes this is normal, why isn't this normal? Why can't I do this? Surely Frank won't care. *Ohhhhh, FUCK*, Frank is going to hate this. Okay, think of why this is normal, and then what can Frank say? Nothing, Frank can say nothing. Opposite, you know it's going to be the opposite, FUCK me, Frank is actually going to fucking hate this."

I spend the rest of the day researching "holding boobs and not drinking", finding heaps of porn sites and rubber dolls, but also finding absolutely fucking nothing. I moan to myself, "Of course I don't." I think, *Because it's MY fucking story and OF COURSE it has to be hard.*

But, oh well, it makes her happy and, fuck me, I think, *I just lied and took away her milk because I couldn't handle fingernails down a chalkboard. So what if she's holding my whole boob that is sitting outside of my clothes like a gigantic skin football? Um, so what? She's still weaned. Still stopping "milky-time", but it's just looking a little different.*

"Nothing to see here." I say this out loud. Emily stops cuddling the "milky" and looks up at me. "What, Mummy?"

"Oh, nothing," I reply. "Mummy is just being silly. What say we go to a playground shall we?"

The day passes by with more "milky" cuddles and I am increasingly anxious about Frank seeing this.

When Frank gets home I busy myself with Emily and put on my 'nothing-to-see-here' face and attitude, which I now realise makes me look like an uptight Mary Poppins.

Once bath time is done and we are sitting on the couch for some pre-bedtime cuddles, she asks for "milky-time".

Frank looks up sharply, his face dark and stormy. "What?" he firmly asks. "I thought -"

"Yes, yes! We have!" I interrupt very quickly and with a high pitched, over-the-top happy voice. (I sound like I've sucked on a helium balloon.) "The milk has all gone; it's been a bit of a sad day for Emily, but she is just wanting to cuddle the milky so she still feels comfort."

I pull the big skin football out of my top. It sits over my top like a huge balloon. She presses her cheek against it, left hand underneath, right hand over the top. She rests happily into it and just watches TV on my lap. She hasn't asked to drink it, she is comforted, she is happy, and yet I feel like I'm doing something wrong and Frank is most definitely contributing to the weird factor.

"So, we're doing *THIS* now?" he asks darkly, and his face tells me that, *Yes, Mum, you are doing something wrong.* In fact, he says it: "It looks VERY *WRONG.*"

I feel my instincts rise, giving me the strength in these dark stormy moments.

..."But *why?!* She's just cuddling it! She feels sad, she's fed for three years and she had a big cry this morning. She asked if she could cuddle it. I told her there's no more milk so as long as she just cuddles it then I'm fine with it. It's *MY* body anyway and if I'm fine with it, then who cares?"

My eyes pierce when I speak from the wild wolf mother of my psyche deep within me.

Frank glares at me, but he backs down.

"Well just don't go doing it in public or anything... It looks weird."

I lighten the mood because I see he's backed away and I don't want to go to bed on a fight.

Marriage class 101: *Never* go to bed on a fight.

"Why not?" I laugh in a jovial I'm-just-joking way. "I can start to normalise *THIS* as well? Hahahaha, can you *imagine* the look on their faces in the food courts?"

Frank grunts at me, and I hurriedly get Emily to bed.

I know it will take him time to get used to it. After all, he wanting me to stop feeding her at six months and look at how well we did – we got to three!

As I put her to sleep whilst she is cuddling my "milky" I reassure her – in case she picked up on Dad's aggressions about this, as I know she is much more alert to our conversations than he or I give her credit for – that she can cuddle "milky" for as long as she wants. I reassure her that she has done such an amazing job breastfeeding for so long and as she drifts off to sleep, I feel a peaceful calm descend on me.

I feel that I have been able to wean her into the next chapter with a solution to ensure my aversion didn't hurt my baby and that my baby is feeling completely supported and comforted.

The next morning there are no tears. The "milky" is cuddled morning and night and a lot of afternoons when tiredness needed that extra physical love.

There was never an attempt to drink from the "milky" by Emily ever again. She went on to cuddle that "milky" for a whole year. Until her brother arrived and, when she saw him drinking from the milky, she did ask if she could have some. I actually said "yes", but when she saw the milk come out of the breast, she said, "Oh yuck!" and never asked again.

Frank did eventually stop making comments about the "milky" sitting randomly outside my clothes. Although his face showed me that he never actually got used to it and once the brother started to feed, he couldn't help point out to Emily that he couldn't believe she cuddled that "thing".

After that first day of no milk being drawn from my breasts, and after feeling that peace descend on me, I started to notice something quite wonderful happen in my relationship with my daughter.

Instead of pulling out my boob as I quite often did if she was upset, I now had to stop and listen to her, start to talk to her, cuddle her and "parent" her into the solution.

I realised very quickly that I was becoming a parent, and the relationship with my daughter got even better. (I wouldn't have believed it if you had told me whilst I was breastfeeding her!)

I was so delighted. *Excited*, even!

Especially when counselling distraught mothers feeling aghast at the thought of needing to wean.

It just gets better! I kept saying, again and again, so excited that my new journey into parenthood was so absolutely delightful.

And it does. It just gets better.

Although some things, for me, got worse.

Chapter 2
MEETING FRANK.

I am sitting at the prosecutor's desk in a court room. It's 2022, and I have my head in my hands: The Magistrate has just deemed my concerns for my children's safety *"not enough evidence"* to put them on the Intervention Order. I loudly and openly moan, *"Nooooo!"* and burst into tears. I direct my tears at this woman who has just shoved another hurdle in front of me.

"My babies," I say out loud and, with that, I drop my head into my hands and sob.

I sob loudly, I sob openly, and the Magistrate excuses herself from the room.

I allow myself the time to cry.

A court clerk plops a box of tissues in front of me and I finally lift my head and grab two from the box.

I am not spoken to, looked at or comforted.

Well, this is fucked, I think to myself.

I press the tissues into the corners of my eyes and I manage to stand up. My legs are weak from all the fight and flight responses happening during the questioning and I limp out of the court room.

I am in the passage way, one door away from the general public seeing my face – my red "I-just-lost" face.

I sink to the floor, curl up like a child and put my head in my knees, covering myself with my arms.

I sob there for a while.

I let it all come out and I allow the darkness seep out of me with every tear.

No one comes in or goes out; I am left to grieve in peace.

I am tormented by the decision, but feel OK after the huge release and the wild woman within giggles that she knows this magistrate felt guilt and that's why she left the court room.

"Fucking *bitch*! She will have her mind changed – I will give her so much evidence she won't sit straight for a week." I feel reassured that all will be well after a call from my lawyer and I retreat to the park across the road to sit on the grass and smoke a cigarette.

I soak in the healing beauty of nature and try to focus on the beauty of my surrounds.

Then it all floods back to me.

The whole nineteen years.

The story of Frank and me.

It's always alarming when I think about how I got here.

Meeting a man, getting married and having kids.

Not something I ever thought I wanted, but, as the years rolled around and my lone wolf existence started to show up as not being successful, I started to dream of "belonging" somewhere.

It's the human's deepest desire, to *belong*.

Brought up by people that didn't understand, see or even so much as like me, I have never ever felt like I fitted in.

The 'black sheep' of both families, I was creatively brilliant; academically I could put my mind to anything and wasn't as ugly as I thought, or was told, I was.

By the time meeting Frank rolled around I was working as a pole dancer at a gentleman's club in the heart of the city.

I actually loved this job. This one provided me with the empowerment of womanhood I had been lacking in my immaturity. A shitload of money (earning potential was endless!) and epic conversations with really decent men. Yes, *decent* men attend strip clubs.

The shit ones usually get kicked out.

Wild and free, I felt like I was at the epicentre of truly discovering life in the big smoke and I was loving every minute.

My second experience on drugs (ecstasy no less) is how I met Frank.

What a story to tell the grandkids.

It's less than a week after my first experience on drugs and I make a new stripper friend that is exciting me.

She is very free, VERY loose and very, *VERY* wild. I love the naughty glean in her eye and she and I have a great time doing pole tricks at the club that night.

We do lots of doubles, earn a *LOT* of money and towards the end of the night she asks me,

"Do you take drugs?"

I am excited to answer, "Yes."

I don't let on that I have only tried it once before.

"Oh, thank goodness – I knew you were cool!" I am relieved I have answered her correctly. This chick looks exciting and I am feeling tingles all over my body. My heart is racing with anticipation and I can't help but agree, "Yes, I am cool."

We finish our shift and she has hustled up a party of sorts for us to attend.

A young man who lives in an apartment in the new high rise apartments of the city has invited us over to keep 'partying' after our shift. He and his friend have been out all night; our shift has finished at 2am so we have only had a few drinks whilst working. We are allowed to drink, but not get drunk, and so we are relatively sober compared to him and his friend who both look like they are at the end of their evening versus us two who are only just getting started.

My new friend is very loud and chatty, I notice with a twinge of annoyance, and as we ascend in the elevator, she is demanding quite loudly to know where and what type of drugs he has.

I withdraw sightly, keeping my pretty smile painted on (it's hard for me actually - I'm usually a Resting-

Bitch-Face type of girl), and I become very, very quiet.

I take all of this conversation in and start to really pay attention to the size of the man and what may or may not be in his pockets. I note the level we have landed on and I quickly look for the fire escape once we get to the apartment. I am on high alert.

I have not done this before – gone back to the home of a customer – and I am very, *VERY* nervous.

I am hoping she isn't too crazy and offered us up at a fee behind my back, I think in a fit of slight panic.

Full service (prostitution) is not where I will ever go.

I already feel the edges of my moral compass wavering with stripping, and have started to allow some line crossing to happen in the club out of, to be honest, sheer fucking laziness.

I cannot be bothered hustling quite so much. Too many nights of "No thanks" or "Not tonight" really knock my confidence, so I start to 'offer more' in the lap dance.

This line crossing is breaking the rules, breaking my compass and breaking my heart.

I am honestly near the end of this exciting journey in my life and am tired of the "game" of trading myself for the money. Yet this new thing, this thing called "*drugs*", is calling me in a way I have never felt called before. So I take deep breaths, clench my jaw and keep an eye out for any people we might not be expecting in this man's apartment.

Not one that hasn't been in a physical fight with a man before, I am confident I can protect myself.

But I am not so confident that I can get out of this situation with a crazy stripper who I only just met.

We enter his high-rise apartment and the view is insane. We can see the whole of the city through his 180-degree lounge window and I think, *Fuck me, this city is beautiful.*

I stop to take in the beauty and am quickly jerked back out of this moment of splendour by the constant, grating voice of my new "friend" loudly asking again, "Where are your drugs?"

"I'm a drug pig," she says proudly.

I don't know what a "drug pig" is, but the way she says it makes it sound yuck and I start to think she's a bit of an idiot. However, I am stuck in this apartment with an annoying stripper and a young man that is probably regretting inviting her back to his house.

I relax very quickly as I note the nervousness around this young man and I see he is more afraid of us then we are of him.

I am alarmed as another young man comes out of a bedroom near the kitchen as I wasn't expecting anyone to be home, but, after he introduces himself, I relax very quickly as I realise that they are both harmless.

This apartment, I discover, actually belongs to the father of the first young man, and he is allowed to live here and study.

"Lucky bugger," I start to speak.

He lights up a little, I think, pleased to hear from someone that isn't just demanding drugs.

We have a quick chat about uni and he is surprised to learn I went to uni, surprised to learn I am not a bimbo, and he is also surprised to learn I am four years older than him.

I am young looking for my age. I always have been: I am constantly told I look at least ten years younger than I actually am.

It's a blessing mostly, but can steer people into different perceptions of me, yielding sometimes frustrating results for either them or me.

He asks me if I want any drugs and I am asking what he has.

He has pills ('E's') and ketamine.

I have no idea what ketamine is, so I just say, "I'd like a pill please."

He only has one, so the four of us divide it into four and have a quarter each.

My "friend" is complaining that a quarter is NOT enough for her and she demands the ketamine.

He gets out what looks like brown powder and I am glad that I am "not into ketamine", which is my response when offered it.

The boys ask if we want to hang around and thankfully my friend says, "No thanks, we are heading out clubbing tonight."

They are staying home they say. So it's a simple handshake goodbye from me, a full-on kiss from her, and they settle back to watch movies and take drugs at home whilst my bubbly friend starts to dial a cab in the elevator.

"Where are we going?" I ask, wondering how long before the pill kicks in.

"Chapel Street," she answers. "There's a club there that I've been to before and it's amazing."

We get into a cab, and halfway there I start to feel really, really, *REALLY* good.

I nudge her, "Are you feeling it yet?"

She is smiling and nods. "Yup, that was a GOOD pill."

I shush her as we are in a cab, but she just laughs.

"Who gives a fuck! We are strippers we can do what we want!"

I laugh too, although I quickly look in the rear view mirror at the cabby to see if he noticed what she said. He appears not to have been listening and so I settle into the amazing feeling that is happening in my body right now.

We pull up out the front of the club. In typical stripper style we get straight in (I am starting to get used to this and I feel very VIP!) and then I am hit with the beginning of the rest of my life.

I stand at the back of the dancefloor after we enter and just stare.

For as long as I can remember, I've been searching for a particular type of music. Faster, harder, louder, deeper.

I have been searching in all the mainstream places, and of course couldn't find it.

But here I am, twenty-six years young, and I have finally found you.

Hello, Hard Trance.

My friend is grabbing at my hand: "Come on! Let's find a podium and dance!"

I love that this club has podiums. As a stripper, I am obsessed with being "on stage". It's something that takes a few years to wear off actually. I love being the centre of attention and if there's a table, a bar, or a podium, I am the first on it during these years of my life.

We are feeling the effects of this little pill and, though it is not as strong as my first time, I am so entranced by the laser beams (these were not at the first club I note excitedly to myself), the hard dance music (again, not at that first club), and the podiums, that the effect feels way more intense.

I am on the podium. I am feeling overwhelmed again by the sexual feelings the pill is evoking in my body and I turn to my friend and kiss her.

I almost feel 'obliged to'; it's like my body is saying, "*this is what you do when you are on pills*". She accepts the kiss and we have one passionate kiss that I felt, at the time, was where taking pills took me.

She laughs but just motions to turn around and just keep dancing.

I ask her if she's okay with me kissing her. I stress that I have offended her.

She tells me not to stress, and yes, it's fine, but she just wants to dance, and encourages me to just focus on the laser beams and enjoy the music.

So I turn around and face the DJ.

I focus on the green laser lights and try to dance to this fast amazing music.

I am interrupted from my awe by someone tugging on the leg of my jeans.

I ignore it initially, thinking that it is someone just trying to sit on the podium and they have accidentally knocked into me. Then the tugging is more insistent.

I look down at the person grabbing me.

It's a tall, brown-haired, brown-eyed young man with a drink in his hand.

"Do you want a drink?"

I have to lean down to hear him properly.

"Pardon?" I ask him. He says again, "Do you want a drink?"

I think about it and answer, "Hmmm... I'm not sure. I'm on a pill and I'm not sure if I'm meant to drink on it."

He laughs. "Is it your first time?"

I feel reassured by his honesty and I am relaxed enough to answer, "Second actually."

"How much did you have?" he asks.

"A quarter," I reply.

"A quarter?" He looks amused. "Are you serious? And you're feeling that good?"

I nod yes, not sure if this is a good thing or not, but I do know that I am anxious to keep dancing to this incredible music.

I stand up and start dancing again.

I'm not sure if I'm doing it right, but not caring either way.

I have my hands in the air and I feel incredible.

I feel a tug on my jeans again.

I look down. It's the young man again and he is handing me a stick.

It is white and it kind of glows in the dark.

"Here," he says as he hands it to me. "Have this."

I say thank you, grab it and just look at it.

"What do I do with it?" I ask.

He laughs, "This really is your first time isn't it?"

"No!" I defend my party honour. "It's my second, honest. But I've never seen these things – what do I do with it?"

"Wave it around," he laughs.

I stand up with the glow stick in one hand and I hold it in the air to wave it in time with the music.

I look down at him to see if I'm doing it "right". He is nodding. "Yep, just like that."

I smile and keep waving it.

Then I realise my friend needs to go to the toilet and I realise I do too.

I jump down from the podium and go to give the man his glow stick back.

"No, no, you keep it – it suits you." He smiles, then asks, "So what's the go with your friend? Is she your girlfriend?"

I look confused for a minute, and then remember the podium kiss. "Ohhhh that! No, she's just a friend. I work with her."

"So you're not into girls then?" he asks.

I tell him that although it's nice to kiss girls every once in a while, for me, at the end of the day, it's actually all about the dick.

He laughs his head off and we talk some more.

He wants to buy me a drink and I want to talk to him more but my friend – who I am not sure I really like that much anymore – is tugging me to come to the toilets with her.

"I don't want to go by myself," she insists.

I actually *do* need to go too, so I excuse myself from talking with this man and go to the toilet.

I groan. The line is HUGE. *This is going to take ages!*

I think about the man the whole time, and when I *FINALLY* get back out, I cannot find him.

I am actually really gutted.

I didn't even get his name!

Nothing eventful happened for the rest of that night. I bring my idiot friend home with me and, high as a kite, I invite her to live with me (...or was it the other way around? who knows to this day). The next day she flies to Queensland and I tell her I will see her in six weeks so she can then move in and be my drug-taking housemate.

I come down badly: my body hurts and I cry a *LOT*.

But I am determined to keep taking these drugs and I am excited about this new life I have discovered.

I keep that glowstick in my car for two weeks and, exactly sixteen days later, I find myself walking straight back into that young man's life.

I'm out on a Saturday night with a friend. I've taken drugs and am wanting to keep going but no one is interested in partying.

I get a phone call, quite randomly, from the friend of a guy I am sort of dating.

It's a 'friends-with-benefits' situation. (I absolutely HATE these situations. Men, *please* do NOT do this to women. It's a complete head-fuck, and it absolutely shreds our self-esteem. Women, *do NOT do this*. He is *not* going to change his mind.) He is high and wants to still keep going.

I am driving home from the club I've been at and I am excitedly saying yes to a new adventure.

"Where are you?" I ask him. He says he is in the Chapel Street area so I come to pick him up. He tells me that there is a club open on a Sunday during the day called "*Evolution*".

"Cool," I say, "let's go!"

We drive to the club, park the car, ensure we don't look too sketchy, and enter this amazing two-storey venue. The club plays the same amazing music that I have begun to love and cherish: Hard Trance.

I tell my friend that I need to go to the bathroom to freshen up and, on my way back downstairs, a young man runs up to me.

"Hey you're that stripper girl!"

I look at him. He doesn't look that familiar, but maybe he is...Did I do a dance for him?

His smile is nice and inviting and I pretend I know him. He says, "Come and say hi to the guys."

I agree and go with him. Something about him is so inviting I think I'm heading home.

I walk into the back area and there on the ground is the brown-haired man that gave me my first glow stick.

My eyes light up. "It's *YOU!*"

I give him a big hug and he smiles.

"I still have that glow stick you know," I quickly tell him.

"Really?" He smiles, and I sit down beside him and we start to talk.

I find we connect immediately and he introduces me to his two other friends, again with the one who had initially found me.

We all decide to put money in to buy some pills together, take them and party away our day.

I remember my friend that I came with. He says he feels sick and needs to go home and I say goodbye without giving a care in the world. These are my boys now, I think to myself.

I feel so completely at home and there is something about that brown-haired man with the dark brown eyes that I simply need to be around.

I ask him his name. "I'm Frank," he says, and I immediately enter his number into my phone and into my life forever.

How things changed.

Chapter 3

THE TRUTH ABOUT FRANK AND ME.

The first time Frank laid a hand on me was around 2006.

We had been together for a couple of years and were the 'rock solid' couple that everyone around us looked to for 'relationship-goals'.

I adored him.

I absolutely adored him.

I just poured all my love onto him and he said it made him feel special and, well, I have a big heart. I mean, when I love you, you just can't help but feel it.

I knew that though he hesitated to be with me (I kind of came with a big bundle of crazy), he just couldn't resist that love.

So much in him changed. He hated PDA (Public Display of Affection), but after being with me, realised he had to deal with it. I was all over him; I was an undeniable force of love that no-one, and I truly mean this, NO-ONE could have said no to.

I believe it was fate. I had had a vision/dream the first night after we kissed that we would get married... So for me, it was easy to just keep loving him, regardless of how little (and sometimes there was nothing) I got back.

But I won him over; I moved in with him a year after meeting him and he eventually opened his heart to my love. Did he truly love me back?

Well who knows? You'll have to ask him but, from what I've read about men, unless they have to fight for that woman, they never truly love her.

And Frank won me sleeping. He didn't have to fight one single bit.

I knew this and yet I still didn't care.

I wanted him, needed him, and my life was all about getting Frank to be my husband.

I believed it was fate and I believed I could love him enough to have him forever in my life.

So we moved in and the happily-ever-after journey began.

With a lot of speed up our noses and a *lot* of ecstasy pills.

We were MAJOR party animals.

We were Ravers.

Big time.

Every single weekend was filled with dance parties.

We had our regular clubs and sometimes they changed, but what didn't change were the friends we partied with and the drugs we took.

Every single weekend.

We took drugs. A *LOT* of drugs.

Frank was great because he was sensible; he always wanted to finish up at the end of a weekend and go to work on the Monday. To be honest, if he didn't have this attitude, I think I'd have become a full blown junkie.

I never wanted the weekends to stop.

My self-esteem was zero when I met Frank, and these parties were giving me so much joy that I just didn't want it to end.

When it came to Frank, sometimes we weren't compatible. I could see that, if I was truly honest with myself, but I didn't want it to be the case. So I pushed it down and used every single trick in my book to have that man stay in my life.

The saying 'Pushing a square peg into a round hole' was exactly who I was.

I knew I was pushing for something and someone that may not be right for me, but I was so determined, it didn't matter.

Square peg? Who gives a fuck, I'll shave some edges off – I will MAKE myself fit.

The first "laying of hands" was a build-up of a year of financial abuse. The money 'thing' really pissed him off. I was the opposite; I couldn't give a fuck about money. I could live week-to-week quite happily.

I wasn't a materialistic girl so wasn't into buying clothes and couldn't afford much anyway.

I was always more interested in spending money on the things that made me feel good, like drinking or, now, drugs.

So once we had our first tiff about money, I shaved the edge off my square instantly and I arranged to have my pay check put directly into his bank account.

That dedication to him regarding money floored him. He was delighted and we got along better than ever.

"See?" I told myself, "That is what you do. Just give him everything, and he will love you back."

Not worrying about losing my self-reliance and sovereignty, by laying myself at his feet, paid off. He could see my dedication to him and I was rewarded. He bragged about it to his friends and they all saw that I was really in it for him, not his money. (Given they all knew I was a stripper when I met him, some of his less open-minded friends had accused me of chasing him for his money: Frank was a saver and had a lot of money in his bank account when I met him.)

But the edges of my squares always grew back and the next thing was my propensity for being sensitive.

I would get offended if someone looked at me the wrong way. I would have falling-outs with people, unable to clearly define who I was in a situation due to lack of emotional intelligence; I would always feel less-than, worse-than, and unworthy. It was easy to offend me, but I didn't know any solution other than to walk away from them. I would love you until you upset me, and then I would leave you.

That was my defence mechanism.

Frank had high values for being everybody's best friend. Still friends with his kindergarten buddies, and having grown up in a small community, he was very proud of the fact no-one disliked him. (Or so it appeared: I later found out some of our mutual friends actually didn't like him as they could see the way I was being treated.)

This was a huge difference of values between us that would always be a big wedge in our relationship.

I was more focused on spending time with people that genuinely wanted to spend time with me. My location issues – I lived a long way away from friends after school – meant that I was always forced to make new friends, which I did easily. However, keeping them was another story.

I was an undiagnosed alcoholic in those early years of life. A typical move for an alcoholic is to run from themselves. So moving from town to town whilst my drinking behaviour got worse and worse (I had no idea drinking was the problem at the time) was just something I got completely used to. I accepted that part of me.

I had boyfriends whose friends I became friends with but, when we broke up, I lost all those friendships too.

Being a lone wolf meant that I was always entering into a relationship solo.

I had to rely on the kindness of strangers - always.

Which, to be honest, always served me well. I'm not a shit person; I am generally happy-go-lucky and a 'live-and-let-live' type of personality. I am genuine and caring and, for the most part, just like to have fun.

But if you hurt my feelings, instead of sticking up for myself, my strategy was to just walk away.

If they loved me, they wouldn't hurt me, I would justify to myself.

Many, many confused friends I am sure I have left behind me, who potentially may never know why I walked away due to my inability to confront and honour the Elizabeth within.

I was admonished harshly, when I would admit my sensitivities. In particular, I would say, "I don't think so-and-so likes me" or "so-and-so said this and this hurt me".

I was told, "It's not all about *you*, the world doesn't revolve around YOU", and then walked away from.

I was left reeling every time. Normally, I thought, I would be the one walking away. It terrified me.

I was so terrified of him leaving me, and he didn't want me to not like him, that we always made up and I would shut up and do as he said.

Frank and I were driving out to dinner one night to meet friends all the way across town.

We were excited and after being together nearly two years we felt like that 'rock solid' couple I truly thought we were.

I felt like I was being the most amazing girlfriend: I was obedient, I was adoring, I was pretty, I listened as hard as I could and shaved and shaved those corners off my "square" relentlessly.

We hadn't had a fight in a long time due to my amazing behaviour and I was feeling blessed.

If Frank was the church, I was attending daily and I was on my knees for him.

Obsessed with pleasing him, I was cutting off the hands of the woman I was growing to become and she was absolutely screaming at me from deep within. I told her to shut the fuck up so much that it made me angrier and angrier.

I look back and realise what that anger was, but I honestly thought it was because I was "coming down" off so many drugs. I was able to have that anger released every weekend via the multitude of drugs and that is why I loved them so much. It staved off the anger from the deep wild woman trying to claw her way out from within.

However, this one night, she couldn't keep her mouth shut and it caught me *and* Frank completely off guard.

I had noticed, in the few years with Frank, that his need to be liked by everyone meant that he actually had no backbone. He was indecisive (I always had to order dinner when we went out for dinner) and unable to have a negative opinion of anyone, except his best friend (which I found to be disrespectful). I actually found it unattractive in him as a man; I didn't know then what I know now about men, but my inner-woman knew that this was a trait that I really didn't like about him.

However, I was trying to push it all down, along with all the rest of the stuff shoved down there.

He asked me what I thought about a certain situation in relation to his family this night as we are driving out to dinner.

I respond by saying, "I think you are sitting on the fence about it."

He swiftly turns to look at me; glares at me, more like.

"What do you mean?" he asks and my wild woman launches without me even batting an eyelid.

"I think you're a fence-sitter."

Before I could turn to look at him, he grabs my head with his big hands and shoves it into my car window. *Hard*.

"*FUCK!*" I grab the top of my skull with both my hands and the wild woman screeches from within.

"Stop the car!" My head burns and stings and I see stars.

They are right, I think angrily. *You actually see fucking stars!*

I am reeling, absolutely reeling. Every single part of my body is shaking. I am frozen, I am angry and I am sad and the wild woman screams, "GET OUT!" So I demand loudly again, "*STOP the car!*"

Frank, cool as you like, says, "Don't be ridiculous, we can't stop here its peak hour traffic."

I am silenced.

I am numb.

We drive in silence towards the restaurant, until Frank asks me to direct him via the maps. He refuses to acknowledge what has happened and my wild woman continues to shake from within.

I sit there. I am frozen, angry, and confused.

I know not what to do at all. He was meant to stop the car, I was meant to get out, and it was all meant to finish here. The wild woman is so angry, yet I do what Frank says, silently moving into accepting what just transpired.

I numbly direct him to the restaurant and as we reach our destination I start to breathe again.

I realise I haven't taken a proper breath since he's pushed me and I start to gather my wits about me.

We find a park and stop.

Once we get out of the car Frank puts his arm around me as we cross the road towards the restaurant to meet with friends for dinner.

I inwardly shrug away from his touch. It's an inward withdrawal though, so I know Frank doesn't notice it.

My soul shrinks back from his touch and I stare at the road in front of my feet.

I notice my feet walking one foot in front of the other.

I feel numb.

I am silent and I am angry and very, *very* confused.

"It's just a fight," he says quickly before he opens the door to the restaurant and we walk inside to greet our friends.

I am looking down at my feet still but realise I have friends to greet.

I lift my chin, put on a big smile, and say hello.

I realise that I am relieved to have cuddles from some loving familiar faces.

I quickly excuse myself to go to the bathroom to gather my shit together.

I check my make-up, check my head for any blood or bruising, and just take deep breaths, gasping the air in and holding myself up by leaning my hands either side of the sink.

I'm staring into the plug hole and breathing when a friend comes into the bathroom.

I feel she has followed me and she asks, "Are you OK?"

She has noticed. I can tell this by the tone in her voice.

I look at her wondering if I should say anything.

I search her eyes and try to figure out how much she knows.

I feel that she is going to be placated with a simple 'Yes, I'm fine'.

I also don't know how to go about any of this. I'm overwhelmed by the decision and am not sure how she will react. I want to focus on gathering myself together before attempting to be brave.

I realise that the desire to leave him is no longer there, and the self-loathing makes me sick.

So I decide not to say anything.

I lie to her and say, "Yes, of course, just doing my make up," and we leave the bathroom to go have dinner.

The entire dinner I can barely look at Frank, but after a few wines – I notice that he keeps them coming for me – he charms me and smiles at me and pays more attention to me than ever before.

I actually feel like I've accomplished something.

"See?" I tell the wild woman, "If I let him do this, then he loves me more. Now SHUT THE FUCK UP!"

I can feel her sit down within, hang her head in shame and fold her hands around the back of her head in defeat. I can feel her loss, but I ignore it by drinking more wine and eliciting the joy of Frank paying attention to me.

On the drive home, Frank apologises for "having a fight with me before dinner".

I feel myself bristle from within knowing that that's not what really happened.

But I say nothing.

He then firmly reminds me that he is close to his family and that if I ever say anything negative about them again, regardless of the context (I recall thinking that he has clearly missed my point), that we will end up fighting like that again.

I accept this. I take responsibility for my part to play in this, and the wild woman moans and sulks deep within. I am angrier at her than ever and I hope she doesn't get me in trouble again.

It doesn't last long.

She's a very strong woman.

Chapter 4

MORE TRUTHS.

With Frank, I was the little girl.

His role was similar to that of a parent to me: I was ticked off, told off, sent storming off for quiet time (this was "me" led, but still, it felt like I was in a "time out" sometimes). He would fire off these phrases regularly to me.

"Don't speak to me in that tone of voice."

"You are rude, don't look at people like that."

"Stop being so sensitive."

"I don't need to explain myself to you at all."

"There is something wrong with you."

"The whole world doesn't revolve around you, you know."

"You're a psycho."

"You're a freak."

"Shut up for once."

"It's no wonder you have no family."

"You are a fucking *cunt* of a thing and I hate your guts."

All the words I truly thought it was a "right" for a boyfriend to say to his girlfriend.

After all, he said them to me. I insisted on staying and loving him, and yet something deep within me was fighting to get out. I just kept telling her to *shut the fuck up*.

The money was "controlled".

The words were being "monitored".

The behaviours "watched".

There was definitely no doing anything by myself.

Life was only alleviated by the relief of the weekend drugs.

The physical violence was only a once-every-second-year thing.

The head into the car window happened and I didn't honestly think he would touch me or hurt me again.

So when we are starting to fight about things, mainly because we are tired or 'coming down', he started to show real anger.

Frank wasn't an angry man naturally; in fact, he was known for being very happy-go-lucky, so the fact that he was so angry with me deeply scared and upset me.

I was incredibly insecure, so much so that I'd regularly "crack it" if a woman so much as looked at him. Yes, I had my deep flaws too. It was a "thing" for me to storm away if a girl talked to him too much. Once in a nightclub, a girl touched his arm – she could see very clearly that we were together – and so I launched.

I grabbed her by the arm and dragged her away snarling, *"Get away from him!"*

I nearly got kicked out, was made to apologise to her, and only did it because my pills had kicked in and I didn't want to leave the club peaking on ecstasy.

He would laugh about this and I think he liked the attention, me fighting wholeheartedly to be his girl, and yet we would argue regularly about this insecurity I had.

These arguments were solved very quickly by reassurance from him that he would never cheat. We had both been cheated on prior to meeting each other, so the faith that he wouldn't deal that to me kept me feeling okay.

I learned to deal with my insecurity with his advice, actually.

After my insecurities nearly upset a lovely birthday lunch with his friends, he sat me down and dealt out the one of two pieces of advice I took on, and still to this day pass onto his children as good ideas from their Dad. No, they don't know he treated me like this, however they are cluing onto why we are not together.

He sits me down in the bedroom one day and says, "We need to talk about your insecurity. It's really driving me nuts and making you unattractive."

My heart sinks, I am flooded with the rush of cortisol coursing through my body, and I instantly think,

He's going to break up with me. I feel my heart sink further and I am finding it difficult to breathe.

He means so much to me I cannot lose him, I think.

"Shave more corners off the square peg, *FIT* into that round hole," screams the inner-child who loves him the most. "He is our ticket out of loneliness - don't you DARE mess this up. He is the dream we had as a little girl: we get to be in a relationship, settle down and have kids; this one won't leave you if you behave yourself. So shut up and BEHAVE!"

I listen to her and I try to calm myself down, not very well, as he makes a comment: "Don't look so scared. It's okay; we just need to talk because it truly needs to stop."

I am still trying to breathe. It's hard to talk and I have such little emotional intelligence I think I even let a tear slide down my face. I am panicked, I cannot think straight but I cannot under any circumstances lose this man, so I say, "Okay, I hate it too. I mean I trust you, but I can't help feeling this way when another girl looks at you or talks to you."

He then tells me he used to feel this way too. He says, "You need to feel like you are the catch, not me. You also need to just tell yourself, every time you feel insecure, that you just don't feel that way anymore".

He admits that he did it himself and, eventually, he was no longer insecure.

I just stared at him, not quite understanding how to put this into practice.

"So, like, just pretend I'm not insecure even though I am?"

He replies, nodding, "Yes, sort of. Basically just say to yourself 'I don't think like this anymore' and eventually it will go away. Trust me – it's worked for me".

We kiss and make up. I am more relieved than anything that it's not a break up. I realise later in life that he has given me a tool to use, not just for my square peg corners to fit into his round hole, but a life tool that I now see as something I would even recommend to a client. Mastering your mind is an incredible weapon to live a happy and successful life.

However, the honeymoon period of me feeling secure and nothing happening again finishes and we have our second violent incident. Only this time I am his fiancé.

We had just bought a new car together. He drove a work van and my car was dead, so we decided to get the Subaru Impreza RX our ultimate "clubbing car". We look online for ages and then he somehow finds out an old school friend is selling one. It is a girl; she owns her own beauty salon (successful), is part of a loving family (values), and is absolutely stunning (brunette – which he once admitted was his preference. Me? I'm blonde-haired and blue-eyed).

We meet her and I know straight away that she likes him. She limply holds out her hand for me versus the usual hug and kiss that I am known for (super loving and friendly) and I eye-ball her. It's a look women give to one another that says: "I know what you're doing, Bitch, and don't even try it – you are dealing with straight up *Psycho* here". She acknowledges the look I'm directing at her and I actually see her physically back away a little.

"Good," I think, "She can feel the intensity of my knowing, and she's intimidated."

I have been told many times in my life that I can have "crazy" eyes.

You may think that this would offend me but, well, it doesn't.

As a victim of abuse from childhood to adulthood, those eyes have staved off who knows how much more abuse and, now, it's giving this intruder a firm push away from my man.

As he is looking at the car and sitting in it, I do the usual chit-chat. I ask about her business and then get over-friendly about how I'd like to use her salon, and become friends with her, and do that whole "let's be friends even though I dislike you" routine.

A thing I would do to ensure a woman who is stepping out of place steps the fuck back in.

You want to threaten my life? Well, let me get all up in your life and see if I can't just straighten this out.

You want in on my man and you think I can't notice it? How about I hang out with you and just see how much integrity you have. This one had none.

Obviously knowing I was doing the friendly routine, I could tell she was physically backing away in front of me, but I could tell she meant nothing but trouble.

Two weeks later I notice a text on his phone from her. Now Frank and I had an open phone policy, both having come from cheating partners we decided it was best to just check each other's phones and it would help us trust being with a partner again.

It wasn't an all-the-time thing that had to happen, but more like: if I'm up at the bench and his phone dings with a message, then he'd say, "Can you check it babe?"

So his phone dings, I pick it up, and it's her.

She messaged him seeing if he likes the car, and would he be keen to catch up for a drink this Friday night? There is a wink emoji beside it. My heart stops and my adrenaline kicks in like a fucking race horse.

I read it out to him and start to really fume.

"I knew that fucking *bitch* would try something!" I snap loudly.

"Woah!" he says, "You don't even know her; I've known her for years - she's a nice girl"

"Who clearly wants you and has no respect for the fact that you have a fiancé. I mean, she fucking met me!" I am so angry that I almost throw down the phone.

"No!" I continue to rant. I am enraged: "That fucking slut – how fucking *dare* she?!"

He gets up and takes his phone from me.

"Would you relax!" He cuddles me and I calm down, sort of. We finish the night by watching TV.

But it's on my mind relentlessly for days at a time.

When we go out clubbing next I vent to my friends. I'm furious. I rage about it and they agree, *she's a fucking Slut-Face-Bitch!* and I am justified in my rage. They also reassure me that he wouldn't cheat on me and I agree. However, I am niggled that he didn't tell her to fuck off...which is precisely what I expected him to do.

A few weeks later and again I am nearer to the phones than he is and again his phone dings.

It's a message again, from *her*.

I fume instantly. My whole body is in a fit of absolute rage.

She is asking him out for a drink AGAIN, with a bloody fucking wink emoji.

I do note that he hadn't responded to her first text.

Which should have reassured me, but I am beyond it. How *DARE* she continue this!

I am now also outraged because, had he told her to fuck off (obviously if he wanted to do it diplomatically he could have), then this wouldn't have happened again and I wouldn't be feeling so angry.

Waves and waves of anger pour out of me and through me, and I am barely able to speak.

In fact, it then freezes me.

He looks up, "Who was it babe?"

I ready myself before answering.

He notices I am not speaking and asks if everything is okay.

"No," I reply through gritted teeth.

"She's messaged you again."

"Who has?" he looks at me. I look angrily at him with eyes that say, *are you FUCKING kidding me?!*

"Oh." He comes up to view the message and give me a hug.

He reads the message and I realise I am shaking.

I am so outraged: How could she do this to me?

He tries to reassure me, saying, "You can see I haven't responded to the first one though, so don't even worry about it - I'm not interested in her."

My brain and emotions ping at an incredible rate. I am so outraged that he cannot see that he should have done something about it – in fact, *could* still do something about it.

I demand retribution. I am in full-blown outrage and am only saved by the fact that we need to go out for another party. Frank jumps in the shower – a great way to shut me up – and I hustle to calm my anger down and pretty myself up for the night. I cannot WAIT to vent again to my friends.

On the way to the party, I decide to shut up about it. I can actually feel a wall go up around Frank and I am also tired of fighting about it; I feel like I'm not going to win this one.

So I turn to listening to light music and having light discussions about the people we are visiting, and we generally have a good night, albeit a big one on the red wine for me. Red wine; the evil equaliser, if I was feeling good, red wine always brought me down.

If I was feeling happy, it would make me sad. If I was trying to be nice, I would always sound mean.

But it also just made me loosen up and this was *NOT* what Frank or I needed to happen right now.

We get home and bustle about getting ready for bed.

I go from zero to one-hundred and start demanding why he couldn't message her back to "stop her texting you".

I get nothing from him. That wall Frank has created is still there.

"I don't want to talk about it, let's just go to bed." He is firm and not too angry but I don't see the warning signs of what may transpire if I don't back down. I've had way too much red wine.

I get up nice and close, the inner wildness angry from the last couple of times he has hurt me and, every time something happens, she remembers and she tries to come all the way out.

I'm close enough to be touching him and I accuse him of cheating on me.

I ask him bluntly, "Are you cheating on me or not?"

He snaps.

He grabs me by the shoulders and throws me away from him towards the end of the bed head. I hit the foot of the wooden bed frame, landing *hard* on my right ribcage

I then hit the floor, and instantly double over in severe pain.

I am clutching my right rib, pain still managing to soar its way through me despite the red wine.

He ignores me and just hops into bed.

I freeze.

I am numb.

I am in *so* much physical pain.

I think, *I have to get out of here*. I crawl out of the bedroom, and then stand and leave the house via the back door. I am completely delirious and I go into the back yard, realising how absolutely drunk I am as it's not cold and I usually feel the cold really easily. The dog wants to follow me and I let it. I think, *I am going to disappear*: all sense of normality has made me slide down into a pit of despair.

"My ribs," I wince, as I try to open the sticky, rusty door of the garage.

I see a pile of cardboard and I bundle it together and lay on it.

I curl up in the foetal position and just stare into the blackness of the garage.

"What the actual *FUCK* just happened?" I manage a thought. Not many are capable of coming.

My fight or flight usually gives me the freeze. I cannot think, I cannot move, and I cannot process anything.

My ribs are burning with pain; no position is comfortable and I close my eyes despite the pain and just try to sleep.

All I know is that I cannot go back inside.

Ever again.

I start to drift off and all of a sudden the door of the shed swings open loudly and Frank asks angrily, "What the FUCK are you doing in here?!"

Again, I freeze. I cannot speak; I cannot look at him. I just lay there.

He grabs my right arm and drags me up. I yelp in pain.

"What?" he spits, "What are you carrying on about?"

I gasp, "My ribs!" They are killing me. He has his big hands wrapped around my shoulders and he is rough and, no matter what gets touched, it hurts.

"Don't be ridiculous – you're just drunk. Now get inside. You can't sleep in the shed."

I fight him off – I am not dead yet, you fucker! I think angrily to myself – and walk by myself.

"What the fuck do you care?" I argue. I'm so fucking angry at him and also at myself (not that I realise this until many, many years later).

"But I'm sleeping on the fucking couch. You've *broken* a FUCKING RIB."

Ah, there she is. *Fuck you, you brute*!

He storms off again.

"Don't be so fucking dramatic," he spits back at me as he goes to bed, seemingly okay with the fact that at least I'm coming inside. Okay with the fact that I'm this hurt.

I get inside and am overwhelmed by the sadness of what has transpired.

I know I must leave, and yet I don't know how to do it.

I don't remember this bit; the red wine was clouding my mind and I was searing with pain, so I am not sure if it was putting me in some sort of shock or not, but I sit down at the computer and email EVERYBODY on my email list, typing: "This is the end, it's time I need to go. Goodbye."

The next day it is business as usual.

I have taken one quarter of a Xanax the night before and I wake up surprisingly chirpy.

Well, not feeling like killing myself as I usually do after getting drunk.

Drinking is not something I do often in my late 20's so I am relieved the Xanax has helped stave off that dreadful hangover.

Frank calls me during work to demand to know: "What the *FUCK* was your email about?"

I freeze. Instead of being angry at him for the rib, I instantly cower into taking responsibility for anything and everything to do with the world and I stop everything to take this on.

"What email?" I am timid and I go on to tell him I don't know what he is talking about.

"You've gone too far this time – you need to get your shit together. We will talk about this tonight," I am scolded and then hung up on.

I am burning up with fright. "*Holy shit*, what the fuck have I done?"

I log onto my email account and have about forty emails from people that I haven't spoken to in ten years, worried about me, asking if I'm okay.

I shit myself again; I am simply flooded with cortisol, my body is jangling with nerves and I'm scared at the fact that I have blacked-out.

I don't remember writing this at all.

The fact I have blacked-out after not 'blacking-out' for seven years has scared me more than the contents of the email.

Yes, the fact that I drank too much scared me more than my ribs being broken, and more than the fact that I was low enough to write a "goodbye" email to my contacts list.

The confusion within is very real.

I put out the 'spot-fires' of concern for my wellbeing for the day, and I start learning how to block emails: I have accidentally emailed my stepfather and I haven't spoken to him for over a year – *shit!*

I get home that night and don't speak to Frank at all.

I am mainly terrified but I also recognise that I am angry at him.

I have made my way home via the doctor's clinic and it is confirmed that I have a cracked rib. I ask the doctor to note it on my file – that my fiancé shoved me onto the bed. This then turns into a conversation about safety for my wellbeing, which has me back-tracking a little as I am nowhere near ready to see I am being abused and I simply wanted the doctor's sympathy. I didn't actually want real help, just a shoulder to cry on.

I get home and sit in the car for a second or two. I breathe deeply and am genuinely not sure how to handle myself. I decide that I am angry about the rib and, if I come at it from that angle, he will not be cross about the email.

Manipulation is a game I have started to use regularly to try to elicit the response I seek. It is hard when I am not sure of the parameters yet.

Some weeks it is okay to be honest, other weeks I need to find a way to be okay with him treating me the way that he does (and has) and then yet still gaining his comfort. It confuses me, and yet makes complete sense at the same time. He is the prize here and my job is to keep him on his pedestal and not let him fall.

If he starts to slip, that's when I notice I get hurt.

I walk inside feeling like I am fuming at him and I decide that I actually require solitude to overcome this.

However, I am feeling so broken and so alone that, once I walk in the door to him waiting for me, his simple act of putting his arm around my shoulders in a gentle way has me bursting into tears.

I bury my head into his chest and ask him why he did it.

"Did what?" he murmurs into my hair.

I am silent.

I rack my brain with what to say and try to push down the wild woman because she has caused this.

"Look what you did!" I abuse her internally, "*Why couldn't you just SHUT UP for once? Everything was going so well and you just couldn't help it could you?*"

I say nothing at all; I can't even deal with any more fights so I just cry.

He holds me in his big strong arms and I pretend they care about me.

I don't really know – maybe they actually do?

Maybe it's okay to get thrown about a bit... I mean, mostly we have been great. Perfect, in fact.

How bad is it to have a head slammed into the car window a few times?

TV remotes smacked out of hands and cushions thrown at heads.

It's not like he's punched me.

...Or drawn blood.

I justify everything that has happened.

I am a fiancé; I am nearly there, the stakes are too high for me to leave.

We get married next year. I am nearly at the top of the mountain and I will *not* give up.

I take a deep breath in his arms and make myself smile. I look down at the ground, still not quite able to look at him, and I ask, "What would you like for dinner?"

Chapter 5

MORE AND MORE.

The broken rib pushes me into a paradigm of acceptance for abuse that I haven't reached before.

I notice it start to change me from the inside out.

I feel a scratching on my insides begin. It is like the wild woman within scratches a day on the wall of my soul; another day to endure being me.

Scratch...scratch...

I ignore her, and push her underneath a heavy blanket of anger and shame.

I then focus harder on my outside goals; I am engaged, I have a steady job, I have steady friends and I am a steady drug taker.

I can do this.

"Fuck off," I keep telling this feeling inside. "Just. Fuck. Off."

I am basically telling my soul to get fucked, every single day.

I am shredding my soul with every decision to ignore it, breaking pieces of myself off and tossing them to the ground.

There are pieces of me in the gutter as I'm smoking a cigarette outside a club, pieces of me in the supermarket aisles when I am choosing dinner for him, and pieces of me just rolling around like tumbleweed. Aimlessly rolling across an open field, no direction, no real purpose except to just exist and roll around, and maybe get abused for being there.

I am already being abused by him, so to be abusing myself creates deeper wounds for me internally and larger cracks are forming deep within my soul and psyche.

During these days, weeks, and months, I become fabulous at zoning in on my physical health and my body is in the best shape ever since my pole-dancing days. I have been doing a lot of work on my outside self, quitting smoking, eating ridiculously well, and I am even delving into attending the gym five nights a week, meditation and weekend yoga.

I even take up running which, if you knew me, is so outside of my comfort zone that I cannot believe I do it.

But even though the work I am doing on my outside self is helping to a certain degree, nothing can stop that internal scratching.

She is marking off those days in my "life calendar", determined to make me feel her.

I do what I do best though, and I ignore her more than ever.

So when the next physical violence occurs, it's just like breathing.

We are heading into another dinner/party with some friends.

We have been a year engaged; we have received club celebrity status amongst the 'crew' and everybody just loves us. They love our "love" for each other.

We always appear to be in so much love and to be honest – for the most part – I was very genuinely in love with Frank. I had him on a pedestal: I knew the stakes were to just keep him up there to avoid my own demise (the demise from abuse, or worse: he leaving me. Yes, that was my mindset – for him to leave me was a worse fear than the abuse. This is what is happening for multitudes of women; the thought of being alone, or having to lose a relationship that on the outside is validated as ideal, means you feel you would rather die if you lost it). And so I fell into that role really easily and I did it really well.

I am a natural giver and lover and also, I have discovered, a natural manipulator.

I was always manipulating a situation so that Frank had a good night with me. For instance, if he bought a new t-shirt and felt good in it, I would then go around the club to people, even strangers, and ask them to compliment Frank on his T-shirt. This, so that Frank would feel so good about himself, that there would be no way that he would leave me. Why would you leave someone that did this for you? But I never wanted him to find out it was me: I felt it was going to work out to be some form of karmic law – if did all these amazing things for Frank, one day he would do all these amazing things for me.

I felt so certain that if I poured all of my love into *him*, that one day he would pour all of his love into *me*.

I never told him I did things like that for him, but my friends knew and most of them thought I was amazing and loved him so much that I would do anything for him.

However, one or two were seeing through it all and would casually mention the pedestal I was putting him on. They are still the friends to this day that called 'bullshit' on the whole thing and still chose me as their friend post-divorce.

So we are driving to a dinner, and we have a conversation about friendships. I know that Frank and I are on different values here. He believes it to be more important to remain friends with people no matter what.

I believe that people come and go, and that if someone treats you like shit that you have every right to stop talking to them.

He strongly disagrees and we are arguing about how this is affecting him, me not wanting to save a friendship over his values of saving it.

I am arguing that he should be sticking up for me and seeing my side, that this person is rude to me and that he ought to take my side. He argues that the person I am feeling hurt by is in a relationship with one of his friends, his friends came before me and that I am causing trouble by feeling hurt by this person.

It's a confusing debate; both of us completely unable to listen to the other, completely worn out from organising a wedding and, of course, we are six years into taking a shit-load of drugs. Our brains are just worn-the-fuck-out.

Then mine gets another bashing.

I am running out of patience with him not hearing me. The scratching propels me to snap at him and I tell him he isn't being a good fiancé and I hate it that he doesn't support me.

He snaps too: *"BAM!"*

My head gets slammed into the car window as we are driving down the highway going at one-hundred.

I hold my head with my hands. I see stars again. *FUCK those stars*, I say to myself.

I grit my teeth and I snarl at him, "Turn around!"

He ignores me and keeps driving.

My voice is low, deeply angry and I have never heard this tone from within before.

"I said, *TURN THE FUCK AROUND*."

He looks at me and starts to look for an exit.

We do a U-turn and drive home in complete silence.

Once we are home, I get out of the car first, slam the door so he 'knows', and walk inside.

I wipe off my make-up and just go to bed.

I say nothing to myself, I say nothing to Frank, and I even say nothing to my friends about why we didn't make it.

He also says nothing. He sleeps on the couch that night and the dog sleeps with me.

The dog has had the shit kicked out of him too. He understands how I feel and yet both of us are powerless to do anything about it all.

We just hang in there, both of our tongues hanging out, panting for a drink of that soul water and anxiously needing just a shred of love.

I stop caring about anything for a *long* while after that.

I continue the facade of my life, but within myself, I need a huge outside distraction to actually begin to feel anything again.

I increase the amount of drugs that I take and I increase the intensity of this show that I am the star of, the show called "*In Love with Frank*".

The best distraction is my up-and-coming marriage.

It is a six year journey for me to get down that bloody aisle.

The perseverance was intense; I endure the abuse and I feel like I have "made-it".

We are getting married and nothing and no one can eliminate the smile from my face.

In fact, I am so happy I feel like I have 'cracked the code' to life and my journey into being a better person steps it up a million notches.

I have been in counselling for about two years since the departure of my biological mother and am feeling good about myself. Frank's constant insistence that there is something wrong with *me* – in terms of why there is abuse between us – is a catalyst for me to want to change.

I am continuing meditating, I start doing the acting courses I so dreamed to do, I am now totally into studying nutrition, and I have quit smoking and continued to exercise.

I am feeling outwardly amazing.

But internally, it is a completely different story: I am nervous and frightened.

I hide those feelings by ignoring them, drinking more wine, taking loads of drugs, and even refusing to talk to my psychologist about it.

I am in complete and utter *denial.*

Yet, the constant memories of abuse were gnawing away at my sense of right-versus-wrong.

Was I doing the right thing?

I continually tell myself to shut-the-fuck-up and ignore the deep sensations that are trying to save me.

I block the internal out as much as possible.

I kept putting on a massive smile and, interestingly enough, I kept feeling like those years were a scene in a movie.

The whole relationship feels like it's a movie, still to this day.

Not my life, not real, and definitely not something I ever thought I'd experience.

Everyone around me, around us, just wanted us to be happy.

I did too but, looking back, I knew there was a warning bell going off deep down inside that I refused to listen to.

The wild woman was moaning at me from deep, deep within, sitting under a shit-load of anger and tears that I refused to allow out as I wanted so badly to have this relationship.

I had made the deal with the devil on this one and sold my soul for societal happiness.

However, even in reaching everything I was striving for, in everything I fought to keep, there was a Divine purpose at hand with me. Is it possible I needed to have that relationship, to birth children within it, so that I could now write these books to help other mothers and parents rise?

I feel it is so.

I am okay with what I went through. I am strong: I am resilient.

Would I have been so had I not gone through such trials?

I believe not.

Nothing is regrettable in my journey to becoming a mother.

I believe that I was fighting for my children, long before they were born.

I believe that no matter how I became a mother, it would have been a fight so that I could fulfill my destiny here on Earth. So it is.

However, now it is time to inspire you, dear mother, if you are reading this and resonating with what you didn't know was abuse. Perhaps you can be inspired to rise and to leave him.

Whatever you think you want, as a woman, you must listen to the duality of your nature.

There is the one who walks the earth: she listens to the worldly desires, fights to have the nice clothes and all the things she thinks she needs. And then there is the one who lives deep within, the one who knows.

This one is spiritual, and this one actually knows what you truly, deeply desire.

You've heard her haven't you?

She's the one that wants to say, "No I hate playing video games actually," when that first crush invites you to the arcade for a date.

She's the one you pushed away to prevent her saying, "Can you please dance further away from me? You are making me feel uncomfortable."

You know she's in there. You can hear her in the aftermath of the trauma and abuse.

She tries to warn you, tell you what to say or do.

But you never listen.

You think you are doing what you need to, but you are obeying what societal construct says to do.

You feel like you finally 'fit-in'. You were always that 'black sheep' because you listened to the wildness within and you used to not give a fuck about how you look or how loud you talked.

And if someone was mean to you, you would happily do a '180' and walk, or even skip, well away from them.

Finding a partner that is society-based and on the basic level started to quieten that wildness within me.

I was told that doing '180's' was not allowed anymore. You can't say, "I hate chocolate"; you have to love it now because *"that's what women do"*.

I had to brush my hair and care if my fanny was shaved and washed.

I had to shave all the time under my arms and also my legs. *All the time*...

I also had to stop farting when I needed to.

I could see I didn't fit in, and the stakes become so very high to gain that *ring*, that *gown*, and that *marriage certificate*. They are too high for me to be me, so I focused on not being me.

So that I could be the *me* I *thought* I wanted to be.

And it nearly killed me.

I walk down the aisle. I honour my goals with a decision to marry him before God and I walk into the next chapter of my life:

The one of becoming a mother...

Chapter 6

ABUSING THE "MOTHER"

We are pregnant.

"More like I am pregnant," my disgruntled wild woman snarls from within when it is announced like that.

She is becoming a lot like a wolf, very snappy and very much protective of this baby growing inside of her.

Once I find out I am pregnant Frank's need to control me steps up a huge notch.

Plus, we have just started renovating the house and he is not quite happy about the pregnancy. Instead, he is mortified and loudly exclaims, "Now I have lost my worker!"

I am shocked at how often he bemoans the loss of me "helping out" and I actually feel so much guilt that I don't rest; in fact, I continue to physically labour and assist with tearing down the back of the house. Until, at around ten weeks, I start to spot (bleed).

It actually takes a conversation with our obstetrician to convince Frank that *"No way should she be doing any strenuous physical labour"*, at which Frank even has the gall to ask the doctor if *He* is going to help him with the extension.

The doctor and I share a look that can only be described as a mutual *"What-The-Fuck"*.

In the initial stages of this pregnancy and – I'm not even joking – the day after testing positive, I get morning sickness.

I am not happy about it as I do not cope very well with feeling physically sick.

I tell Frank how I am feeling and am accused of "putting-it-on".

"Bullshit!" he snaps at me. "You literally just found out you are pregnant; I bet you read about it in a magazine and now you want me to bloody give you back massages and be your servant. Well, that's not happening."

I am mortified again. Honestly, I am truly *mortified* when this new chapter of my life not only doesn't stop the abuse, but *amplifies* it.

Many of my friends that can see through the bullshit of Frank and me have always believed that once I am carrying his baby, this will soften him, make him respect me more.

But it doesn't.

I am always lighting a candle of hope and I truly hang onto that hope that he will change when the baby comes.

For now though, I literally cannot eat. I cannot walk. I can barely move.

This baby is clearly healthy, says the doctor, as morning sickness is a sign of a healthy baby.

But I do not cope with how I am *feeling*: it feels like a hangover 24/7.

The only way I can avoid feeling it is to sleep.

The poor dog, my only friend and ally in all of this, is now too "smelly" for me to go near and so the poor darling is missing my cuddles and pats. I honestly cannot cope and Frank is spending most of his time moaning about how I am now no longer cooking for him.

I can barely eat and for days and weeks I can only eat pineapples, ginger beer and dried biscuits.

I dry-retch over the toilet daily and yet nothing comes up.

I am so miserable I can barely function and Frank has me in tears most days, which isn't too hard, as I'm usually crying anyway thanks to the massive shift in hormones.

He uses the tears to verbally abuse me and, with the renovations in full swing, he uses that as extra ammunition to continue to berate me for 'getting pregnant at the wrong time'.

We are in a very dark place.

I actually retreat to sit in the shed in the mornings to cry in peace and also to get away from him.

I am crying all the time – at work, in the car, at the shops, just bloody everywhere.

I cannot stop crying.

I also start to become abusive myself and find myself in fits of rage at the strangest moments.

One day, I'm lining up at the car wash, and a P-plater ducks in front of me which takes my place in the queue.

I go from nought to one-hundred and see RED. I slam my hand on the horn and just hold it.

I am fuming, my eyes glaring at this car full of young, free, little assholes that just took my spot at the car wash.

I refuse to take my hand off the horn and I just glare at them.

They look at me and I get out of the car.

Full, angry, pregnant belly approaching them.

"You took my spot!" I am practically growling, snarling like a wolf.

They don't hesitate: "Sorry!" one of them squeaks, and they jump back into the car and quickly drive it around to join the back of the queue.

I wash my car and start to feel the flood of emotions run through me. I am so angry I have no idea why I have taken it out on these kids so aggressively.

In fact, the extreme anger worries me to a certain degree; I have never felt quite so angry in my life.

I start to cry as I am washing the car and this feels more like me.

Tears, come on out! There's so many of you down there, I muse to myself.

It's like seven years of tears all being released.

One must also remember, that it's probably a massive come-down too.

I was potentially a week pregnant and trying cocaine for the first time.

I hadn't had a break from drugs for seven years.

The emotions that I was repressing regarding all Frank had done to me were simply pouring out and my pregnancy was healing me more than I ever realised.

However, all I feel is sickness, sadness in my heart, and intense stress.

We need to move in with the in-laws whilst renovating and I am deeply troubled when I pick up on their intrusive nature. They have no boundaries. They do not listen to our wishes with the dog who has gone from being an inside dog to an outside one and I cannot get out of that house fast enough.

Frank actually starts to slow down the renovations when we move in with them and I panic that I am going to be stuck having my baby there. It is something that continually gets suggested as a good thing and something that I resist very firmly.

I take over project managing the renovations and I am on the phone at work calling tradies every day to speed up the process.

Frank is working a full week for someone else and every weekend on the home, which has turned into him working nights at the house as I am *NOT* having my baby with those in-laws if it's the last thing I do.

So we get the house hustled before the baby arrives and it's time to move out.

I am seven-and-a-half months pregnant.

I pack all our stuff from the in-laws' home and as I am packing my bags, they *demand* to help me.

It is one of the most confronting moments of my life.

My mother-in-law walks into the bedroom we have been sleeping in, saying, "Now, I know you don't want our help, but we are here if you need."

I say, "Okay, thank you. Yes I am fine to pack by myself."

So they sit at the dining room table, situated where they can look at me walking from the car to the bedroom and they both just watch me.

After doing a few trips from bedroom to car, I get cornered in the bedroom.

"Why won't you let us help you?!"

They both tower over pregnant and alone me. I feel scared and attacked.

"I just want to do it by myself. Why can't I move my own things by myself?"

They both berate me for being independent and not wanting their help.

I burst into tears and the father-in-law rings Frank and starts to yell, "She's crying now and won't accept our help. You better come back here there's something wrong with her."

I have been accused many times whilst living with these people that "there is something wrong with me", and Frank will always sit back and say bloody fucking nothing.

This is a new level of abuse, I muse.

I stand up, tears streaming down my face and I insist on *NOT* receiving their help, *especially* after this bullshit 'let-us-help-you-so-we-feel-good' routine.

They carried on at the engagement party, they carried on at the wedding, and they carried on at the baby shower.

I have had enough of their intrusive ways and I storm out, saying nothing and receiving

"*There's something wrong with you!*" being spat at me again on the way out by my father-in-law.

I jump in the car and just drive.

I drive to a friend's house. Actually, I barely fucking know her, but she is the only one I can think of at the time.

She isn't home. I don't ring her and I don't know where to go or what to do.

I sit in the car for at least an hour, in the driveway of a person's home whom I have only just recently met, and I am frozen.

I have no family of origin to turn to, my best friend lives a long way away, and my other friends are all still taking drugs. I am alone, pregnant, and I don't want to have this baby with its father.

I absolutely hate the way his family treat me. I hate that he doesn't stick up for me and I am mortified that I have basically been abused for not accepting help. It feels absolutely insane, but because I have been told so many times that I am "too much" and "not enough" whilst pregnant, I am not sure how I really feel.

I am not sure if what and how I feel is actually *right*.

I start to think there must be something wrong with me.

With that resolution in my mind, I start the car, knowing I have nowhere to fucking go anyway, and I drive to our newly renovated home to face the music with my husband.

I pull up into the driveway, and take a deep breath.

"Fuck," I think, "this is going to be hard."

Already knowing that he will be upset with me about storming off from his parents, I am tense and prepared for the scolding that I know he will deal to me.

I just hope he doesn't hit me while I am pregnant, I think darkly.

I know that there are so many years of anger within me that, if he hurts the baby, I will possibly kill him.

I find him in the spare bedroom and just wait in the doorway for him to finish what he is doing.

He glances around, sees that I am there, and says nothing.

He waits until he has finished what he is doing. It's a tactic I notice he likes to use.

Making me wait, ensuring he lets me know that he is going to prioritise what he is doing over acknowledging me, *especially* if I'm in trouble.

I feel my heart racing. *Fuck*, I think. *What if I pass out?*

I actually start to wish I would, and escape this reality for a minute or five.

Get taken to hospital, beg to stay there. I am wondering if they would actually let me stay there when I am snapped back to reality by Frank's stern voice.

"Well, what have you got to say for yourself?"

I stare at him. I fucking hate this bit, hate how he speaks to me as if I am a child, hate how he doesn't have any empathy for me, and it's just "them" versus me and "they" always win.

"What have I done wrong?" I retort, defending and justifying myself immediately. (I'm always on the defence.) "What is so wrong with wanting to do things by yourself? Why on earth can I not just ask to be left alone? I just want to be able to move my own things into my own home by my own self."

"You," he angrily spits at me (he had started nice, however this is escalating quickly and I start to freak out), "have upset my parents, THIS baby's grandparents! My family means *the world* to me; if you are hurting *them*, then you are hurting *me*... which means you are hurting MY BABY."

I stand there and take it, let the words smack me in the face like they always do, allow the anger to soak itself in and feel the wash of adrenaline course through my body.

I then realise that he is waiting for a response.

I actually cannot talk for a while.

The constant conflict is too much; I try to fight back and all I do is cry.

Frank stares at me. It's not unfamiliar for me to cry and ordinarily he hates it, but I must have looked so damn broken that this time he softens a little.

I just stand in the doorway and cry, and cry, and cry.

"I don't know what to do," I say, and the tears flow and I start to sob louder and louder.

He moves towards me and I flinch initially, but then I realise he is going to hug me.

I lean into the hug. I need nurturing so badly, I actually don't care where I get it from.

I allow this man, the man who hurts me so much, who appears to not care about what I want and who I am, to comfort me with a hug.

"What do I do?" I ask again. "I just want to fix this."

"You need to go and talk to them," he says.

Oh FUCK! I think in dismay. *This is going to really, really fucking suck.*

I look up at him, take another deep breath and say, "Okay."

"Good girl." He smiles at me and cheerfully quips, "See? We'll get through this."

It actually sounds like he is saying it to himself in part, so I just nod and leave the house.

I grit my teeth, clench my jaw, and wish like fuck I had a cigarette to smoke.

This is going to be fucking *awful*.

I get back into the car, drive straight back to the in-laws' house and face the music. Again.

I walk into the house and they are still where I had left them about two hours prior.

My father-in-law glares at me, but manages a "What are you doing here?" and my mother-in-law feigns surprise: "Oh, hello!"

I'm not an idiot, I think. *I know he's rung you to let you know I'm coming over.*

"Hi," I manage, "can we sit and talk please? I'd like to make things right."

They makes movements of "fuss" and "pitter-patter" and "fudge" their way into pretending that this is a new concept for them and me. (It's not: I've been spoken to many times by these people who simply cannot understand a person who requires personal boundaries and her independence.)

We sit down at the table. I am at the head with them on either side of me. (It's a power move, I later recognize, as that wild woman within shows her strength: *Fuck it*, she says, *If you're going to abuse me, then I'll sit at the head of the table to receive it – now come at me, fuckers!*)

"What did you want to talk about?" my mother-in-law asks in the sweetest voice she can muster.

I inwardly roll my eyes. *Oh, just want to discuss how fucking intrusive you both are,* I think to myself, but of course I don't say it.

"I want to make things right here," I say, "What do I need to do?"

I then hand it back to them, give them the permission to launch into all the things that I do wrong.

They do, and there are many, many minutes of me being told I am "too different", "have bi-polar", "too emotional" – "I'm *pregnant!*" I snap back at that one, that I "need to accept their help because that's what good families do" "we know you don't understand because you haven't come from a good family", etc. etc.

I sit at the head of the table, and allow the abuse to wash over me, smack me in the face, the sides of the head, and right into my heart.

I place my hands on my stomach and protect my baby from all this bullshit.

I just breathe through it all and let them have their say. My wild woman smiles somewhat:

"Good girl," she says to me, "take it all in, let their abuse make you stronger. You will have your day."

I feel reassured by her and notice that I can actually hear her say something I agree with for once.

I tell her, "I know, these people are fucking assholes. I will *not* let them beat me."

I finish up with allowing them to help me. I put on the fake smile and pretend that all I want to do is to be a part of their family; I make peace and then drive back to my newly renovated home with my mother-in-law following behind me.

We walk into the house together and find Frank.

He looks stern as he sees me but then his face lights up when he sees his mother. I cringe inside thinking, "*What the actual fuck?!*" I actually feel queasy.

His mother goes over to him and gives him a big 'this-is-a-display-in-front-of-her' hug, then places her hand around me drawing me into a sort of group hug whilst proudly telling him, "We have sorted it all out."

I groan and fume inwardly, "More like *I* sorted it out, you fuckers."

But I say nothing: I manage a sweet smile and I allow the emotional abuse to wash me clean.

He squeezes his mother's shoulder and tells her that he is so happy.

He nods at me and then proceeds to show his mother all the work he's done on the home.

She is admiring his work and chitchatting away, so I go back to what I am here to do and that's move the fuck in to my new home.

But in my mind, I am worried about birthing this baby.

"These fuckers are going to try to take this baby away from me," I moan inwardly, and I hear a cry from deep within my soul.

Their lack of boundaries grates on my independence like a constant spiritual cheese grater.

I am actually sore from deep within at the lack of respect.

I hate it so much but cannot see any way out of this.

My inner child starts to panic. *I am so unhappy right now*, she says, and I respond: *...But isn't this everything you always wanted?*

Chapter 7

THE BABY ARRIVES.

So I have done it; I have survived the courting period, I 'nabbed my man', I got that 'ring on my finger' and I 'walked down the aisle'.

I even managed to get a new home and get pregnant. It's all I was striving for.

So then *why* did I feel so FUCKING sad?

I realise, after the months of stress with being pregnant, coming down off years of drugs, and also the constant battles for independence from the in-laws, that I need to just focus on this baby.

I surrender to the 'nesting' period and get my new home ready for my baby.

I finish work, I do pregnancy yoga, which is a blessing for my tightening hips due to my huge girth (I put on 35kgs with this baby), and it honestly feels like I am ready as I ever will be to become a mother.

The day I am due is the day I give birth.

"This baby better give me a good night's sleep: I'm gonna be *soooo* pissed off if I'm up all night in labour," I declare the night before the birth.

Famous last words and incredible poetic justice for a whiney pregnant woman.

That baby didn't sleep through until she was two-and-a-half.

I know right?

Fuck!

But she did let me sleep until five AM, when, with a sudden uprising from bed, I felt "something" happen in my knickers.

I went to the toilet and checked my undies.

There was some gooey stuff and it was a bit red.

I thought my waters had broken, and, though on reflection understand that that was just my plug coming out, I *knew* that I was going to have a baby that day.

The minute I wiped, I felt a twinge of period pain in my uterus area.

Oh, that was the one thing I DID know – that contractions feel like period pain.

Okay, cool, I thought, *now look at the clock and time it.*

I watched the clock.

Precisely five minutes later that next period pain begins and it was harder. MUCH harder.

Ooooh! I think, "Wow, okay, well I've had severe period pain since I was sixteen. I can handle this, however I think I need to have a shower and get dressed before I get into hospital."

And I woke up the hubby to tell him we were having a baby and got in the shower.

When I got out of the shower and he still wasn't up, I told him in my 'don't-fuck-with-me-I'm-pregnant' voice to get up because I'm not joking we are having a baby and perhaps he can make himself useful and ring the hospital to tell them we are coming? Because the contractions are five minutes apart and stronger every time.

I then blow-dried my hair.

Yes, I did that.

I remember bending over to get some volume in my hair and feeling a contraction and an overwhelming sense of *"Fuck, there's no turning back from here"* swept over me.

The realisation that my life was changing forever dawned on me greater than actually finding out I was pregnant, and I kind of freaked out and wondered if it was too late to stop it. And of course I knew I couldn't, and I freaked out even more for a second.

Until I realised I needed to finish my bloody hair and get to hospital ASAP.

I then started going to the toilet.

It's 5.45AM and I'm sitting on the spare toilet, needing to poo, and I can't move off the toilet.

Hubby is ringing the hospital and trying to convince them that we need to come in.

«*What the fuck are you doing?!* **Get the car started!"** I yell from the toilet.

"They need to know this, this and this."

I politely tell him (scream) that I know what I'm fucking talking about (lies all lies) and my contractions are now two minutes apart and I'm on the toilet needing to push what more convincing do they need to know?

They hear me in the background and agree with him to get me in there *tout de suite*.

We battle about five contractions in the car. I find pressing against the floor of the passenger seat and swearing really helps and we make it to hospital without a baby coming through my legs.

We walk into the birthing suite (a flicker of annoyance crosses my face: *where's my fucking wheelchair? They get them in the movies*). "Didn't you ring ahead?" I snap at hubby and he says, "Yes, yes, we just have to walk."

The tension is huge, inside and outside of my body.

We have a beautiful Fijian midwife looking after me and when I lay down she says she's going to see how dilated I am.

No-one warns me about this.

I think she's going to peek at my vagina and just "look" with her eyes.

No, no; they "look" with their fingers.

When she puts her fingers in there a whole tonne of water pisses out and I all of a sudden need to poo.

I tell her this.

"Okay," she says, and produces a kidney dish.

Oh My God.

"NO!" I am horrified. "I need to do it in the toilet."

She tells me I may be pushing out the baby in that toilet if she lets me do that.

And so I do my first birth poo (the poo ladies – yes, yes, yes, you *MAY* do a poo) in front of her and my husband, whom, up until I was pregnant, I never even farted in front of.

I am *mortified*. I apologise again and again.

Then she says I'm three centimetres dilated and no, it wasn't a baby and it *was* just a poo.

And I'm thinking, "*I fucking KNOW it was just a poo!*"

I feel like I'm unheard from the get-go with this hospital.

I get taken into the first birthing suite and given a mild-tempered, quietly spoken, no inflection in her voice, monotone-as-fuck, way too underachieving midwife.

The contractions are one-and-a-half minutes apart and I am finding that screaming helps when they come on.

The midwife couldn't be more quietly spoken if she tried.

It's like she's trying to be 'Whisperer of the fucking Year' and she just keeps saying really (un)helpful stuff like, "Oh, perhaps you could calm down a little."

Then she directs it to hubby, "Can you tell her to perhaps take it easy?" and, «Do you think you'll need any medication?"

I swing around to face her, which I remember is hard, because I'm straddling the hospital bed like it's a horse.

"Well that DEPENDS. How LONG is this going to take?" I ask her (scream, really).

She looks appropriately startled; was that spit on her face?

"Ohhh, who knows? It could be hours..." she trails off as I look like I've been punched in the throat.

"Hours?!" I gasp; the mortification in my voice is heavy in the air. I glare at her and my eyes cannot be more wide open. I'm terrified.

"Oh yes, it could be a day."

I snap at her quickly, needing a faster solution, "Well then, what are my options?!"

My tone of voice suggests very strongly that she is a complete Idiot and I am about to fucking punch her.

Why does she insist on whispering today?

I feel like telling her to speak up, but then a contraction kicks in and I scream downwards onto my racehorse hospital bed.

I smack away the hubby's hand as he (un)helpfully and frighteningly tries to assist me: "Don't touch me!"

A Scottish midwife comes boldly into the room and demands to know, "What is going on? I can hear you from the hallway."

"I am *HAVING A BABY!*" I snap back at her.

She asks the hubby if I've been like this the whole labour.

I ask, "What do you mean *'like this'*? THIS is a contraction and it *HURTS*!"

She takes over as hubby slinks into the corner of the room and she demands I face the back of the hospital bed. I'm up on my knees and she sticks the gas in my mouth and starts coaching me through a breath.

She then tries to rub my back and God bless my pregnant in-labour-cotton-socks if I don't smack her hand away from there too.

I feel hubby smile with relief; "Oh she doesn't like that," he tells her helpfully.

I won't bore you with the rest, but the end result involved an epidural, with one leg being completely numbed so that Hubby had to actually hold it whilst I pushed.

Oh NO. He'll never sleep with me again if he sees her come out! races through my brain.

And after an hour of pushing, my beautiful baby girl was born, flipping the table on my current existence and birthing within me the most incredible opportunity life has given me yet – the role of *Mother*.

I have literally just pushed out my first baby and she is plonked on my chest.

Let's talk about that first breastfeed – the one that for some bloody reason, I had no idea was about to happen *straight after birth*.

Because I was quite pissed-off that during my pregnancy everyone was talking to me about my baby, when, in reality, it becomes all about your bloody boobs and how to breastfeed.

Seriously, I'm looking forward to cuddling my bundle of joy and yet *holy moly* it becomes all about boobs out and chest-to-chest and chin-to-breast.

Being milked by a midwife (note: how NOT to breastfeed) was an experience that bordered on porn and the look on both mine and Frank's face was that of pure horror.

This feels so wrong, but we are in a hospital, so it must be okay, yeah…?

Let's stop right now.

This is *NOT* okay.

If it's NOT okay outside of the hospital, it's NOT okay *inside* the hospital.

Too many horror stories have been relayed to me over the years while counselling new mums on how to breastfeed, and this quite frankly shocks me.

It's called "Informed Consent" and you learn about it in First Semester Health School. Even a dingbat like me learnt it. So please medical people; get with the program and *stop* doing stuff with our bodies and babies without asking us!

Rant over.

So my beautiful newborn baby is plonked – seriously, *plonked!* – on my chest…How was your baby given to you?

They are slippery little suckers though, so maybe the midwife just kind of dropped her?

"Here ya go, love!" (*PLONK!*)

After locking eyes on this incredible new soul that flipped the table of my life in one split second, she starts to peck at my chest, bobbing her head back and forth like, well, a bird really.

"Ummm..." I search for the midwife who is still down my other end either trying to get the placenta out or stitching up my fanny.

"What, um, is my baby doing?" I laugh with nervous anxiety. *What-the-fuck is she doing?*

"Oh, goodness! She wants to breastfeed! That's quick; she's a go getter isn't she?"

She wants to WHAT?

Breast? Feed?

I had envisaged a few hours of relaxing and having the blood washed off my chest at least....but I have to breastfeed her?

How do I breastfeed? When was someone going to teach me this?

I instantly regretted skipping the second antenatal class to eat chocolate at home because Frank didn't want to come since he had to go to the races with the boys, and I felt a wave of "*Oh-My-God! I can't do this*" wash over me.

I ask for help and the midwife just moves her near my boob and my baby starts suckling.

"*OW!*" I internalise this, but then feel proud instantly.

It's like the world has slowed down and I forget about the blood and the antenatal class, and just marvel at what this baby is doing.

I am breastfeeding, I think, completely in awe of what my body is capable of.

I am in awe of what *I am* capable of... In awe of what *this baby* is capable of.

Then Frank comes over: "Mum and Dad are coming down."

My blissful state stops straight away.

I panic internally. *What the actual FUCK?*

I look at him, "But I just gave birth!"

"Yes," he says, "and they want to see my baby."

I note he says "my" baby and I feel a growl of anger from deep, deep within.

The wild woman is waking up and she is going to launch.

I tell her to shut up.

I recall being dragged into the hospital to see his brother's wife after her second and I remember thinking: "Fucking poor love, we are visiting her and I swear she's just spat that thing out".

I recall seeing the look of exhaustion on her face and now realise where she got it from.

I mean, I've just given birth and I'm to *entertain fucking visitors?*

"No," I insist, "please not tonight – please just give me a night with her."

"Too late," he ignores me completely, refuses to acknowledge that I have even spoken, "they are on their way same with my brother and your dad is coming in too."

"Oh great," I think, "he's going to invite the whole fucking town next."

I am still trying to breastfeed my baby and after about an hour, they pull her off me to weigh her.

Her eyes are locked on mine.

She never stops looking at me.

She has bright blue eyes, and I'm marvelling at how incredibly like me she is.

She is still getting wrapped by the midwife when the first set of visitors come in.

Fuck me. I realise I've still got blood all over my chest, I'm not wearing any undies underneath the hospital sheets and I am absolutely mortified that they are touching my new baby, the baby that *JUST* came out of my vagina.

Watching them touch her makes me feel like I have been raped.

My soul is screaming; I am dying at this feeling.

My sister-in-law comes in and I grab her hand tightly. *Surely, surely SHE understands?*

They did this to her too!?

I say to her, "I have blood still on my face."

That is code for, "Can you get them the fuck out of here?"

She misinterprets like a true indoctrinated member of their family.

"Midwife, can we please have a face washer?"

I am given a face washer and my heart sinks.

"Oh, fucking hell, I am completely unseen here!" I cry inwardly.

Soon the room is full of the intruders. My baby is being unwrapped by the mother-in-law, I instantly wish to kill her and I feebly say, "Please don't unwrap her." My voice is unheard, I am ignored, and I feel like I don't exist.

This feeling, that I am merely the provider of a baby for THEM, continues for many, many years as their begrudging daughter-in-law.

They are intrusive in every single way and every child I produce, they call *THEIRS*.

It *grates* at my soul.

The family spends at least an hour raping me of time with my precious daughter and, from that moment onwards, I internalise and ignore that incident completely. I actually *hate* Frank then and there.

I don't consciously know it, but it is in writing this book that I realise that that is where it truly began.

The respect that I so thought I would get from him, after providing the baby, is not there.

He couldn't even give me one night.

That resentment sits there, fuming, and takes years to acknowledge and process. It nearly kills me before I see it.

After they all fuck off, and the midwife can see that I am overwhelmed by their intrusive ways, she asks me if I am okay.

I shake my head at her. *NO*.

She holds my hand, squeezes it, and tells me I can have a shower now.

As I press my head against the shower wall, I reflect that I have never felt so violated in my life.

I have actually been abused many, many times, and, in that moment, I would rather a gang rape than someone take my newborn baby away from me.

I am overwhelmed by the protectiveness that is pouring out of my soul. I hurry out of the shower when I hear her cry and I simply *cannot* wait to have her back in my arms again.

Once I have her back in my arms, it's a breastfeeding bonanza.

She certainly *IS* a go getter and she insists on feeding every hour.

I mean it – every gosh-darn hour!

It's fairly exhausting, but I don't know how to breastfeed or what to do except just keep putting her back on my boob whenever she gets upset. So for thirty-six hours I do just that.

Don't get me wrong, I love it; after having so many people take her off me in that first sacred night, I am cherishing her need to be ON me all the time.

This brought my milk in like a Queen, and I was a gushing fountain of breastmilk on the thirty-sixth hour.

It's once the milk came in that I truly knew I could breastfeed.

I couldn't believe though, that these incredibly *huge* rocks on the front of my chest were once my breasts.

Rifling through my make-up bag in the hospital bathroom, I was trying to find some lip balm to pop on my cracked nipples.

I mean, these babies were *sliced*.

I had two deep slices on each nipple and they looked like split cherries sitting on the Rock of Gibraltar.

After enduring the constant feed-feed-feed routine (she also hated me to put her down) we reach day four in the hospital.

I am meant to go home by now, but I'm using my acting skills to show I am really, really nervous about leaving the hospital, just in case I want to stay one more night.

Also to avoid going home to Frank and his molesting parents, as I have now discovered that I *hate them all*.

I'm sitting by myself after *again* being shown how to breastfeed and attach my baby – *For fuck's sake!* I'm thinking, *Please let this work* – and the midwife respectfully (this one is not the one that milked me) leaves me to try alone.

I pull down my bra, hold my baby girl to latch onto my left breast (I even remember which breast it is, that's how profound this moment was for me) and she opens her mouth wide. I remember to draw her into my chest and sit up nice and straight like a good student, and she latches on.

NO PAIN.

My eyes go wide with love. I feel the rush of milk come down my breast (the Let-down) and I see her swallow.

The sun is shining into the hospital window to my right and I hear angels sing.

I am in a new dimension right now and, with the sleep-deprivation and delirium of having birthed a *HUMAN BEING*, I am open to all that life is.

Suddenly overcome with a feeling of love and how quite simply *wonderful* this is, I think to myself, *Oh yes, I need to teach mums how to do this*.

And that was the beginning of my Mission in life – to teach mums HOW to Breastfeed their babies; to save the world, one boob at a time.

However, I had to save myself *first*.

Chapter 8

THE ANGER ARRIVES.

I get home, have my new baby in my arms and I sit down on the couch, and *EVERYTHING looks different.*

I remember the vastness of the space around me. My head felt like it was a pin on my shoulders, tiny amidst the enormity of what just happened.

I just had a baby.

I had felt overwhelmed by my mother-in-law consistently over-stretching visiting hours in the hospital, her constant "pop-ins" outside visiting hours completely pulling the rug from underneath my new mum bliss. However, I launched into my "if you can't beat 'em, join 'em" campaign with her and invited her to stay with us for a few days once I arrived home.

Yeah...I did that.

What the fuck, said my inner wild woman, *are you doing?!*

This is the bitch we want to kill, not love.

I realise now that it was such a loving act to do this; I am truly proud that I really did try taking the loving high-road, however reading and writing this book has triggered-the-fuck out of me (thank you healing) and I am proud that I am a lover, not a fighter.

Even though I am fully embodied as the wild woman, I still marvel at how much I did to try to foster love and connection amongst that majorly ill and dysfunctional family of narcissists.

So I'm in my new home, new baby in the car seat in the lounge room, and I'm feeling like a needle in a haystack. Why does everything look so different?

I feel the silence swallow me up.

I will never forget that silence.

It was like a blank page in a book. You turn the page, and the next one is...*Blank*.

You look at it quickly, fleetingly, or for longer, but you still look at it and regardless of how many times you look at it, it's blank.

Continuing to look at it prolongs the blankness of it all, prolonging the silence of words.

There's just a big, fat page of *nothing*.

That's how I felt walking into my house again, with my new baby in tow.

I was facing a blank page.

And it lasts, until the baby cries.

And then the new chapter of my life began.

I had only a couple of minutes of blank page until my beautiful avid breastfeeder decided she wanted more milk and so I positioned myself on the couch in the lounge room and got both boobs out (classic first time feeding position for me: I was thinking, *Oh well, I'll get them both out just in case*) and started to feed.

Every time I looked at her damn amazing face, I swooned with love, over and over again. How could this baby possibly be mine?

My newfound bliss was hampered, as always, by Frank.

"Bloody Frank," I think. "Who-the-fuck is this guy? And *how* on earth did I tolerate his shit for so long?"

These admonishing phrases are what my inner-wolf-woman says; the outer-me plays the game I've been playing for seven years.

Only this time, my tone of voice starts to strengthen.

He feels it; he resists it, and instantly tries to squash it.

...By starting a fight.

Day two we are home and he criticises me for making his parent's feel "unwelcome" in the hospital.

I stare at him.

"Are you serious?!"

My tone of voice is not one either of us are used to.

His eyes flicker with the knowing that I have changed.

After he berates me with his usual "They are my family and mean the world to me and if you hurt them you hurt me" routine, I snap back something about "respecting my boundaries" which gets ignored, and I deal with it by storming off from him.

Unusual...

We are both alarmed by *my* storm off.

I don't usually storm off: I usually cry, which I DO eventually do. This particular fight does end with me in Frank's arms again, sobbing about how overwhelmed I am by having made a baby and how I just wanted privacy.

Bloody hormones.

But something has shifted in me.

I am growing stronger, and I know, as I peer at my sweet baby's face, that it has something to do with her.

We pitter-patter along as parents and simply co-exist for six weeks.

I am focused ten-thousand percent on my beautiful baby girl. She is a frequent waker but I truly don't give a fuck; I just want to hold her all the time. Frank keeps telling me to put her down because I'll "spoil her" which jangles against my instincts and I concede at night times when I put her in a bouncinette which is placed between Frank and I on the floor between our two couches.

Her head is constantly turned towards me, and so-much-so that she develops a flat spot on her head that the maternal health nurse picks up on and asks me about.

The flood of tears begins and I realise, after speaking with the nurse, that it IS okay to pick up my baby. She ventures a query: perhaps I am not getting along with my husband?

No shit, I think, *I fucking hate this dude.*

I look her in the eyes and reassure her that we are fine, and that we have always been fine, and that I just need more information so I can 'show him' what is okay.

She refers me to several resources of information and I start to look into attachment parenting and the breastfeeding association.

By week ten, Frank is more than just a little bit pissed off.

The baby won't be settled by him; she only wants to be on me, she breastfeeds all the time, I am a little sooky about not sleeping, and I am clearly turned well *off* Frank.

I have literally roundhouse kicked that stupid, tall asshole off that pedestal I had him on and placed my baby in his stead.

I feel purpose-driven for the first time EVER in my life and, though I am tired, I am in complete bliss as a new mother.

Except for this idiot man that keeps demanding my attention.

I get accused by his family of ignoring him and not 'letting him have a go' of the baby.

Like it's something you have a TURN of, I groan inwardly.

"She's not a toy," I boldly tell them, "she's *my* baby."

"No!" it is spat back at me. "She is *OUR* baby."

Every visit to their place is torture for me: she is taken off me and walked away with.

Every fucking time!

She gets unwrapped, picked up and taken away from me.

If she cries, she doesn't get handed back.

It's a fucking nightmare for me and for her, and I resent and eventually resist going there.

A weekly visit to his parent's had become a requirement by Frank – after all, they are *his* baby's grandparents and I am not working and it's my duty, etc., etc. (*Blah-blah-blah,* my mind computes this as.)

I fucking hate it.

I start to avoid going to the shops I know they go to. In fact, I literally turn my entire world upside-down to avoid seeing these people so that I can have 'peace-of-mind' and just enjoy being a mother.

So after resisting, and pursuing my sovereign path as a mother, Frank has had enough.

He is tired of not feeling supported by me (*Right back at ya, buddy!* I think), he tells me I am not behaving like a good daughter-in-law to his parents (*but they are cunts*, I say to myself), and he accuses me of turning his daughter against him.

We have this argument in the evening, not the best time to be slinging words over a baby in her bouncinette. She obviously starts to cry and I move towards her.

He puts his hand out as if to shove me and says, "NO! I will get her."

I am alarmed and become very, very scared.

Shit! I think, *what is he going to do to her?!*

She is crying and he picks her up to comfort her, but he is so angry at me there's no way he will comfort her. She cries even louder.

"Fuck you!" he yells at me whilst still holding her.

"See? I can't even comfort my own baby because of you, you fucking cunt!"

I am freaking out, inwardly urging him to just put her down, frightened he's going to hurt her.

I have my hands out to hold her and he ignores me.

I don't exist.

He gives up in anger and puts her down in the bouncinette, purposefully ignoring my outstretched arms.

I rush to pick her up and, to his mortification, she stops crying instantly.

His face darkens in a way I have NEVER seen before and he kicks the bouncinette across the lounge room.

"FUCK!" He storms out of the room and I am left holding my daughter, shaking with fear.

I stand there for what seems like an hour.

I am frightened he is going to hurt us. I cannot move. I don't know what to do, I don't know where to go, but all I know is I don't want to be here, be near Frank, be near his fucked-up family.

I realise she wants to feed, so I peer down the hallway. I believe Frank has left the house to go for a drive and I relax slightly and sit on the couch to feed her.

I am overwhelmed by tiredness once I start to feed her and I decide to sleep on the floor of her nursery.

I literally sleep on a blanket on the floor and have my hand resting on her up inside the cot. I am not up to speed yet with co-sleeping, yet this isn't far away. I shut the door in case Frank comes home, and I truly hope he doesn't.

After the 'bouncinette incident' I decide to try a different tactic.

I go around to his parents' house and try to enlist the help of his mother.

I recall my GP saying that one method of dealing with overbearing in-laws is to enlist or recruit them for support. This can sometimes overturn a relationship or, at the very least, you may get the result you need for your child regardless of having dad's support.

If he is a mummy's boy, then, if mummy says yes, he is bound to.

I didn't think I had married a mummy's boy until I became a mum and witnessed him collapse and turn back to his family of origin.

This is covered in the following workshops Rise of the Parent.

In my experience as a counselor to literally *thousands* of mothers, I have noticed that men either *Collapse* post-birth, or they *Rise*.

This is mainly due to how well they have managed to "work on themselves", or have been raised to believe in themselves, pre-birth.

It has nothing to do with his family of origin (although they can very well hinder his ability to rise and also encourage his ability to collapse, if collapsing is what they themselves did) and has everything to do with his capacity to "handle himself" in any given situation.

Does he sink back and retreat from conflict?

Or does he toughen up and rise to the occasion?

I must admit, the warning signs were there for me the whole time; I should have seen that he was a collapsed man. But I mistook his abuse of me as strength.

Silly me! I admonish myself like I do, and I get ready to begin Operation MIL (Mother-In-Law).

I stride boldly into their home with my newborn baby the morning after Frank has kicked a baby seat across the lounge room and they are surprised to see me.

Mostly because I know that they know I am making them feel uncomfortable because they are intrusive fuckers.

It is this aspect of themselves that no one has ever held a mirror up for them to see, except me.

So they feel uncomfortable around me, as I do them.

I get through the usual bullshit of niceties and then launch into what had occurred the night before.

I explain everything. I even sink into how it makes me feel emotionally, not because I am feeling it at the time, but gauging to see if it will elicit some sort of sympathy or empathy from her.

It doesn't.

In fact, she uses this situation as a way of justifying his behaviour towards me.

"Well, you *do* need to let him do more with the baby," she instructs me.

I am quiet.

Oh fuck, I think to myself with complete dread. *This shit runs deep; these guys are truly unable to see themselves. They are sick to the core.*

I want to vomit.

I want them to never have anything to do with my beautiful baby and I start to pack up my things to leave. I know this is hopeless and I just want to get out of here.

"Are you leaving?" she notices my moves to bolt. "You just got here."

I look up at her. I am anxious to run, I am flooded with panic. The fact that she cannot see how bloody dangerous her son is actually starts to jangle some nerves and I get scared again.

"Oh I forgot I have to do something," I lie.

"What is it?" she questions.

I am fumbling with the baby clothes and I feel hot panic rush over me and I just need to get out of there. *Why the fucking questions?*

She knows, I think, *she fucking knows I'm scared of her and she's going to kidnap my baby and-*

I stop myself from catastrophising and take a deep breath.

"Oh, just a library baby thing I want to sign up for," I lie again and finally gather all my things and make a very hasty exit.

I cringe when they kiss my baby's head (I feel molested whenever they do this) and bolt for the car as soon as they take their grubby hands off her.

Ewwww. I feel ill when they touch her.

Their sickness is deep, like a deadly disease that might be caught.

I resolve in the car on my way home that there is NO WAY that she will be my ally.

They are too far gone and my best bet is to just change my life to avoid them as much as possible.

So the bouncinette incident kicked off a year of intense pain, lots of verbal abuse and yet for me, it was the best year and worse year of my life.

I was so in love with this little girl, she was absolutely everything to me. I adored her, I cherished her, I nurtured her and she filled my starving heart with so much love and joy that I was buoyed into every day by it. The abuse was something that started to strengthen me too.

My motherly instincts were strong and the more he abused me, the stronger I got.

However, I was not strong enough to leave.

I had grown up in a broken family and there was no way I was handing my baby over to him every second weekend.

No way was I handing her over to anyone at all.

So the rollercoaster ride was one I held onto.

When my baby was four months old my mother-in-law was openly telling her to "stop looking at your mother".

When I broached this subject with her, to stop her saying this as I felt that it was mean, she absolutely lost it at me. (I had approached Frank first and he told me it meant nothing and not to worry about it. I asked him outright to actually say something to his mother, to which he said "No".)

My mother-in-law accused me of not liking her, denying that it meant anything, and of course the fight was just as I was about to leave my baby in her care for a wedding I didn't even want to go to.

All I wanted to do was stay home with my beautiful baby; I just loved her so much.

So I have just had a fight with my mother-in-law who denies that it means anything, even though it triggered her to yell at me, and then I have to put on my make-up and go out to a wedding.

The ups and downs were so extreme. I couldn't believe I still had my head on straight.

Then there was the walking away with my baby: Every time I saw her, *every single time*, my mother-in-law would walk away into another room with my baby.

I'd hand her over outside, and next minute Mother-in-law has disappeared inside with my baby.

I hand her over in the lounge room, and next minute Mother-in-law has disappeared with my baby into the fucking laundry.

It was a constant hand and chase, hand and chase.

My baby cries, Mother-in-law wouldn't give her back.

One time, I was actually feeding my baby: She cried as I was taking my breast out of my bra and my mother-in-law walks over and has the audacity to take her out of my arms.

"I'll look after her," she states firmly. My baby was twelve weeks old by then and that actually placed Operation *Avoid* MIL into overdrive.

I quickly and *very* firmly took back my baby (boob swinging in the wind, mind you – No, privacy is NOT an option here) and very decisively told her, "I am feeding her, thank you."

The amount of times my baby was held away from me whilst she was crying and walked away from me was every time I saw them.

So it got to the stage where I'd be up all night, anxious *as fuck*, prior to a family engagement.

I could barely handle it, and meanwhile Frank was like the fucking Lion King, holding his baby up proudly to all the jungle: "See what I did?"

NO, I would grimace internally, *see what* I *did*.

I instantly hated that cartoon after giving birth to my baby and if you have taken any sort of red pill in life, you would hate it too.

So the walk-offs, the lack of support for me from hubby, and the open baby snatching was taking its toll.

I wasn't eating properly and I had sunk down to a very small forty-five kilograms.

The doctor was worried about me. She was on my side and felt like this family was very sick.

Not respecting my wishes was making my wild woman angrier and angrier.

Not without my daughter, I would think, remembering that movie with Sally Field, who fights to keep her daughter from being essentially kidnapped by her ex-husband.

I felt like I was living my own version of this movie.

A woman who was just fighting for her rights to *hold her own fucking baby!*

By her first birthday, Frank and I hated each other openly.

We spoke poorly to each other and avoided each other as much as possible.

The night before her first birthday, we had the biggest fight of the year. Although it was nothing compared to what was to come a few weeks later…

Stress, he didn't cope with: this man was so collapsed it shit me to tears.

I couldn't believe what a fucking *SOOK* he was, and I copped it time after time if I dared him to "Man Up".

He moaned and bitched and whinged about how many people were coming to the party; instead of being *a Man* and taking control, he constantly threw all the stress at me, and then complained about me to his Mummy.

The further into motherhood I got with my new purpose and responsibility, it meant that I had no time or tolerance for his bullshit and I was losing *ALL* respect for him.

I know, you would think that I would have lost it already, with all I had already been through, but I guess my tolerance for pain is large and my heart is even larger.

I genuinely loved the man, and kept forgiving him over and over again.

He wouldn't apologise as such, but I just wanted this family to work out so badly that I stayed.

And stayed...

And stayed...

It's what you do for your kids, I told myself.

The first birthday is okay...

Yeah, nah - it's stressful as fuck: there is HIS family outside down the back and there I am, left inside with my daughter, a belly full of champagne and friends that have heard what my year is like. It is written all over my face and you can also see it on my skinny frame; I am fading away, my eyes are blackened underneath and my jaw is sore from gritting my teeth.

Two weeks later it's Christmas.

I am not even speaking to Frank by then. I can barely handle the stress he has put me under from the birthday party. He had insisted I do absolutely everything.

The most he could do was clean up the bottles in the back yard.

I even took the fucking bins out. This man was killing me and the further we got into this, I just leaned closer to my daughter.

I have no idea what I'm going to do with myself but all I know is this: *it is not without my daughter.*

Chapter 9

Boxing Day.

There are a lot of memories about Boxing Day from my past, mainly to do with being shuffled from one parent to the other when I was little, remembering the fuss on the media about cricket matches and now, this particular one.

This is a Boxing Day I will never forget.

I don't think my daughter will forget it either; unfortunately it will be burned into her subconscious… If she ever does regressive therapy when she is older she may recall what she saw daddy do to mummy.

I hope she doesn't, although, some days, I hope she does. He doesn't fucking deserve her love.

We are driving home from Christmas. It was so stressful for me; I felt so anxious and lonely I even "phone-a-friend" for emotional support during the day. I have been snapped at by the mother-in-law, ignored by the brother- and sister-in-law, and I try to just focus on spending time with my daughter.

I fucking hate this day, I keep thinking.

The niece even offers to watch my daughter so I can "go outside with the others".

The thing is, I don't want to go outside with the others and I mumble something incoherent which I later get into trouble for. (I tell her I'm not the sort of mum that wants to leave her child, something along those lines anyway, and I am later told-off as she was "only trying to help". There's that family disease again: we just *HAVE TO HELP*.)

We attempt to talk on the way home but my anxiety is through the (car) roof, I am feeling awful and he starts to get cross at me for being anxious.

I've "*ruined*" Christmas with my anxiety, he accuses.

I am feeling this inner-woman start to rise up, but I'm too anxious to pay attention. All I know is that she is telling me that there is something very, *very* wrong here.

If I am anxious about something, why am I getting in trouble for it? I think.

Shouldn't I be getting nurtured and supported?

The juxtaposition is spinning my head sideways. I'm not sure what to think and I get a little scared which further fuels the anxiety. Who is this person? I think, and I am reminded of my head getting slammed into the car window. Twice.

I start to feel edgy, there is something driven about the way he is poking at me this day.

I have said my piece which is to simply explain that I felt anxious all day, but now he is drilling me about "*You* not liking my mum", "*You* not joining in with every one", "*You* not letting the niece babysit".

"*Your* anxiety ruined Christmas".

It's a torrent of abuse all the way home, which is an hour-and-a-half drive.

I let it wash over me like I do, and I absorb all the horrible things I am meant to be.

I take it on and this time I try the peacemaker tactic.

I tell wild-woman I am tired, the anxiety has worn me out, and I need to just make peace and rest.

There is a car to unpack and toys to put away and, yes, I know – I will be the one to do all those things.

As we pull into the driveway of home, I am mid-way through telling him that I actually *DO* like his family, and in fact I would like to go camping with his sister like they offered. But as soon as the car stops I feel it:

"BAM-BAM-BAM-BAM-BAM-BAM!"

He is hitting me with his fist wrapped around a water bottle.

My right arm, my skinny right arm, is taking the full force of his frustration at not having married a doormat.

His frustration at not marrying someone who just shuts-the-fuck-up and does whatever he says.

The frustration that he is not my daughter's favourite.

I endure the beating for at least twenty hits and then he pulls away and gets out of the car. I realise he is going for my daughter so I launch out of my seat and meet him at her car door.

It is closed.

I stick my hand up in front of me and say very loudly, "*NO!* You will LOSE HER if you touch her."

I have no idea where the words come from. I am barefoot from the car ride and I am exhausted from the first year of motherhood, but all I know is this: if I let him touch her, I will probably kill him to get her back off him.

He backs away. He can see what he has done to me in my eyes, and I know we *BOTH* feel the strength behind my voice. He walks to the house towards the front door.

I grab my daughter; she is crying but soothes when I pick her up.

I grab my phone and realise it is FUCKING FLAT.

FUCK, I think, *Of course it's flat!*

I am barefoot and I stumble into a run. The police station is about two kilometers away and that is where I am headed.

I am trying to start my phone, holding my daughter in the other arm, and running barefoot away from my life.

He cries out from the front door, "NO!"

I turn to look at him.

Then he starts to cry.

I am shocked. *Is he crying?!*

"*Please!* No, come back! I'm *SO* SORRY."

I just stand and look at him through the bars of the front fence, looking into my prison, and only a flat battery shy of freedom.

It was my sliding doors moment. I truly believe that if my phone had been charged, I would have gone straight to the police.

But I am enamoured by his collapse. This time, he is collapsing *for* me, not *because* of me.

"Please," he begs, "Please, come inside. Let's talk."

His pleading is not like anything I've heard before.

I am captured; my heart opens, like it does and I choose him.

I always choose him, I think to myself.

I actually find my heart opening so much to him after his apology that I find myself taking care of him during the rest of the day.

He behaves like a child and I take care of him.

He lies on the couch, collapsed physically, and I wipe away his tears and sit beside his head and stroke his forehead like he is a child.

I reassure him that everything is going to be okay.

I reassure him that we will be okay.

He just lies there and listens to me.

I stroke his head and he just stares at the ceiling. After a while, I feel awkward.

He is saying nothing.

I feel expectant for more apologies. I realise I am waiting for him to reassure me.

The reassurance from him doesn't come, so I ask him if he wants to be alone and he nods 'yes'.

So I leave him to do my chores. I unpack the car and fuss around the house, and even settle our daughter for a nap.

Then he mentions the traditional Boxing Day party we always attended pre-baby, and states that he feels like going.

He asks me if I want to come.

I freeze.

It pushes me back a step mentally.

What the fuck? I think to myself, and then take a mental summary of what has been happening between us during the day.

He said sorry, yes, but *who* has been nurturing *who*?

I start to feel a little queasy. I then realise I would like the space from him.

I want to re-calibrate what just fucking happened and also just spend alone time with my daughter.

Nothing brings me more joy than this incredible little girl.

I say, "No, I'm too tired."

He says, "Okay," and off he goes.

I say goodbye and think, *This is good, this is as it should be...he needs to be with friends to help him through this.* I assume he will tell them what has happened, they will tell him it was very, very wrong and that he will come home and I will have more apologies and tears of sorrow from him to help nurture me.

I end up going to sleep. He hasn't come home and I get a text message saying that he will be home in the morning as he has drunk too much.

Strangely, I feel pleased he is having a good time, hoping he is recalibrating and feeling into what has happened and will come home very apologetic and sorry.

Then, I think to myself assuredly, *Then, he will comfort me.*

I go to sleep with my daughter, realising I need to sleep on my left side. My right arm is very sore from the beating. I push the pain away and load it onto the wild-woman again.

She is tired too and doesn't fight with me; we are both exhausted and we sleep deeply that night.

He comes home the next morning and I greet him with an anticipation that is never met.

My expectations for apologies and nurturing die, along with my faith that this man is who I thought he was.

I ask how the party was.

"Good," he says.

I ask if he said anything to them about what had transpired between us and he says sharply, "NO, why would I?"

I crumble within.

My heart closes over and I groan inwardly.

Fuck.

What do I do now?

Every time he hurts me, I justify staying. There is my great love for this man, genuine and large as my heart. I simply adore everything he is and everything he is not.

I accept the abuse every time, and I push it down for future-me to deal with, not realising the internal scars that are forming deep within.

I also have an inner-child that has been woken up by the threat of divorce.

No, she firmly folds her little arms across her chest: *NO WAY are we doing that to our daughter*.

I agree with her. My upbringing in a broken home was less than pleasant – it was downright nasty, and even though I now realise it was two toxic parents, at this stage in my life, I am certain that it was just because they were divorced that I was so damn broken.

Inner-child was winning this one and I fully agreed.

I must stay with him at all costs. *Not without my daughter,* I kept saying to myself.

I did research online about forgiveness. I read about how to overcome feelings of betrayal.

I started to talk to my doctor about the incident and then one day, after about a week of him still showing no signs of apology, out of sheer desperation for redemption, I ring his friend who is a police officer.

His wife answers the phone and I tell her everything and she suggests they could come over.

I tell Frank they are coming over. He is not happy about this, but I tell him it needs to happen.

The tone of my voice again stops him in his tracks and he agrees, albeit begrudgingly.

Frank's friend counsels us with this: "First of all, you must decide if you want to stay together.

Then, if you do, this must never happen again. Is this clear?" He turns to look directly at Frank when he says this. It makes me feel slightly better. I am hopeful he is about to say more.

We both nodded.

But, that was it.

No scolding, no big dramatic: *"Why on earth would you treat your wife like that?"*

No: *"I can't believe you did this to her."*

Nothing more than *"don't do this again"*.

Just, "Make a choice right now, and stick with it."

I am silent after he says this.

I am frozen, sad and broken and cannot believe there is no more apology.

But they are all looking to me to respond.

So I say, "Okay."

They resume conversation, changing the topic amongst themselves and I just sit there.

Not sure what I've just agreed to, I feel completely numb inside and I am not sure what is up or what is down.

So when they leave, we are left with the elephant in the room. Again.

Another week passes by and I'm not exactly sure what starts it, but a fight ensues.

It is verbal this time, like they usually are, but by the end of it he is in my face screaming abuse, calling me names and pointing his finger in my face.

I would have been okay with that; yes, I was okay with that, and actually very used to it.

But I was holding our thirteen-month-old daughter.

It was frightening, and my wild-woman had enough.

"*GET OUT,*" that deep, wild voice growled at him. "Just GET the FUCK *OUT.*"

He does.

He hops in the car and drives off. I have no idea to this day where he went.

I am assuming his family home, only three kilometres away. I take two valiums, prescribed by my doctor after assessing the large bruise on my right arm, and then once they kick in, I ring my closest friend.

She has just had her first baby, only a few months old, and I calmly tell her everything.

"Fucking hell," she exclaims, "What are you going to do?"

I ask if I could stay with her for a week or so.

She agrees of course, and I pack a few things and drive to the city.

My friend lives in a tiny two bedroom apartment and puts up a single mattress on an old fashioned steel spring fold-out bed.

It was also their junk room, so I feel like I was being squeezed into a closet.

Yet I felt safe.

Just me and my baby girl, with someone that loved me and saw me.

I stayed a week.

I told him he could see his daughter the following Saturday for two hours in the morning and that was all I said.

I was done.

I felt exhausted from the constant abuse and the constant fighting.

But I didn't know how I was going to do it. I didn't know how I was going to leave him.

I couldn't go anywhere; I had no money, no job and no family to go to.

My friend's closet room was not a long-term solution and I knew I only had a few weeks there at most.

I wasn't strong enough to kick him out. He was so attached to that house that I didn't want to "break him" by making him sell it.

But I honestly had nowhere to go.

That Saturday morning, I take Emily back home to let him see her for two hours, and his father drops around.

I say a quick and terse 'hello' to him and I genuinely don't want anything to do with him so I walk out of the lounge room door quickly, to hop into the car and drive away to kill two hours.

As I am reversing out, Frank comes running down the driveway.

"Wait!" he pleads.

I stopped, hoping all was okay with Emily.

"What?" I was numb; my words have no expression for him anymore.

I feel completely defeated.

But I was soon to feel much lower depths. This was only the very beginning.

How low can you go? Rock bottom is sometimes very, very deep for some people.

Mine is a fucking coal mine.

"Please wait. Please don't go. Please. I am sorry. I was angry. I don't know how to handle all of this. I am trying, I really am, please. Don't go. Come back home to me, please."

He has his hands on the car door and I look at his hands.

Hands that for so long I had loved and admired for the hard work they did; hands that I now feared.

I look down at my own hands. They are petite, long-fingered and ones that continued to move and hold and strive to nurture my firstborn baby.

I clasped my hands together. I remember just wondering why, during this moment, I was thinking about the hands so much.

I was scared: scared of what I was going to say next, scared that there was no going back.

Terrified I was always going to put myself last.

I take a deep and very shaky breath in.

"Okay," I let it out, and if it wasn't for the birth of my son three years later, I truly would have regretted this.

He smiles, he asks me to come back inside and I stall.

"Wait," I say before getting out of the car. "No: you have to promise things will change in the biggest way."

He stops and looks at me, "What do you mean?"

"You have to tell both families what you did to me, and you have to apologise to my father."

He looks at me.

He pauses.

I continued to explain, "Because if someone did this to Emily, wouldn't you want them to apologise to you for hurting her?"

He looks down at the ground and after a breath he looks up at me again.

"Okay. Done."

I perk up. "Really?"

"Yes," he replies, "Really."

"Everyone," I say again, "Even your sister."

"Yes," he replies. "Everyone."

I drive forward and I park the car.

Then as I get out, I walked into a new chapter of my life: *the solutions-focused marriage*.

Chapter 10

MY SON ARRIVES, ALONG WITH A LOT MORE ABUSE.

We kept on keeping on as a married couple and yet something was bugging me: I felt un-nourished by his only two apologies. I didn't pursue the "telling the families" thing yet, but I was still feeling unsafe by the lack of nurturing.

So I inquire at the local church about joining a playgroup.

I wasn't religious: I didn't have anything against churches and having been to an Anglican grammar school for high school years, I actually enjoyed the hymns and safe feelings surrounded my experiences at church. But realistically, the reason I went to church was that it was the only place I could think of that I might feel "safe" in.

Life was very dark for me.

I went to the playgroup and started enlisting the help of a "higher power" to take care of me and Emily. We, Frank and I, move towards a family unit and have deep conversations about what we want for Emily and as a family.

I also move towards having a real career and, after qualifying as a breastfeeding counsellor and taking on the role of Group Leader at the local breastfeeding group, I then apply to study nursing.

I get accepted and by the age of two, Emily's parents are co-exisiting without too much angst.

I have appeased Frank to stay at home due to taking on full-time uni study, and this means I do not have to hand Emily over to the in-laws and go back to work.

I study for nearly a whole year, getting high distinctions and enjoying expanding my academic brain again. Then something shifts in the stars and I realise I want another baby.

I am alarmed at the intensity of this feeling, and felt it was quite poignant that it happened to me in the same space of the house where I had felt it prior to Emily arriving.

I clutch my stomach and look up at the stars.

Woah... **the feeling is** *intense.*

But this time, I don't tell Frank.

We had reached some sort of co-existence; I can manage to tolerate living with him and at times I start to like him again.

But we had both decided that having another baby was off the table.

However, this intensity is very strong: my son is clearly asking to come through, so I sit with the feeling for a few months before eventually telling Frank.

...But not before I start the plan to move to another town.

I know I will have this baby, well before telling Frank, and yet there is *no fucking way* I am having it near his parents.

I plant massive seeds to move location: we find a town near the beach and, once we find a home, I tell Frank I want another baby.

I time it perfectly; we find a home, put in an offer and fall pregnant.

You're welcome, I tell my unborn baby. *I cannot wait to meet you away from the baby snatchers.*

We do a *lot* of counselling before the baby arrives. I am terrified at having the same intrusive experience I had with Frank and of course I am afraid of the actual abuse starting up again.

Therapists tell him he has not left his family of origin for me and my daughter. In fact, three psychologists tell him this to his face. He denies it again, and again, and *again*.

I start to worry.

I am only buoyed by the fact that I find out I am having a son, and then the antenatal depression sets in. Explained in detail in *Rise of the Mother*, I struggle to keep my sanity after receiving a flu shot whilst nine weeks pregnant. It was needed because I was doing a nursing placement in an aged-care facility.

When my son arrives, on his due date *just* like his sister, he is born into meconium waters.

If the hospital hadn't had such strict after birth rules – I had to wait six hours before going home so they could monitor the baby – he would have ended up with cerebral palsy.

He had swallowed meconium and needed it suctioned out of his stomach.

It was the scariest moment of my life.

I am back in the maternity ward after getting a migraine. I am holding my son's hand through the humidicrib, as they are monitoring his breathing after scanning his lungs and seeing fluid on them. I then hear a Met Call over the loudspeaker which is calling on a paediatric doctor to attend special care nursery just after I have left my son there.

I sit up in bed, thinking, *I hope that's not my baby.*

Soon after that thought, my maternity ward door opens and a nurse with a wheelchair appears.

"I need to take you to special care nursery," she says.

I freak out: My heart races and I sit in the chair even though I feel sure I can run, but she won't let me.

The corridor goes on forever and she refuses to speak to me.

Fuck fuck fuck fuck FUCK, I repeat over and over again.

The minute we get there I demand, "Is he okay?"

It feels like an eternity that they answer me, and it is a "yes".

I almost collapse out of the chair. I move around to see him and the doctor tells me he has had a "fit" and that it may be epilepsy and she'll refer me to the children's hospital, and so on.

When she leaves me with the nurse and my son, she speaks to me.

"Don't worry about her," she says. "He just choked when we were sucking the meconium out of his belly. He went a bit blue and then he was fine. It's going to be okay. Your son is fine now; we got it all out."

I nearly collapse with relief again, but then I realise I am not going home for a while.

My daughter! Not without my daughter.

I ring my stepmother, who I don't really like, but trust more than my mother-in-law, and ask her to come look after my daughter, two weeks shy of four years old.

I explain everything and she agrees.

I then ring Frank and tell him what is happening and that I have arranged my stepmother to stay with Emily.

During that moment, he even has the audacity to argue that his mum is closer and I feel my heart close again to him.

FUCK, I think, *Again! This is going to happen AGAIN!*

I am right.

The journey post my son arriving is classic intrusive, abusive Frank.

I am abused within four weeks of my son arriving and the first six months of his life consists of me building up muscle to leave Frank.

My son is four months old and I decide to get away from Frank's silent treatments – dealt out mainly because I'm daring to ever say I am a bit tired – and I'm in a rural area visiting my best friend from the small city apartment.

The in-laws are also holidaying there.

I have not arranged to see the in-laws: It's not expected of me at all, but I do the "right thing" upon hearing they are holidaying in the same area. The family disease of "obligation" is rubbing off on me. I hate it, but I obey it. After all, Frank is so much nicer to me when I pretend to fit in.

We head over for a swim in the pool at their caravan park and after our swim, I ask the in-laws to watch my baby son whilst I get my daughter changed after her swim.

When I get out of the change rooms, I go over to the pram and there is no baby there.

I am instantly alarmed.

I look up at my mother-in-law. "Where is he?" I ask, looking worried.

She giggles and says, "We sold him."

I stare at her. It's not funny.

"No really, where is he?"

She realises I'm getting upset and answers defensively: "Oh, we thought he was getting cold so his grandfather took him back to the caravan."

I glare at her.

I demand to know why they didn't tell me.

"Because he's safe with us," she replies.

"But you don't just take someone's baby without telling them!"

I am angry. Angrier than ever: *I honestly cannot believe this SHIT, these disrespectful FUCKS!*

"It's not someone else's baby, it's *our* baby!" she retorts, very defensively.

I glare at her and spit, "You are so disrespectful! I honestly cannot believe this - he's only four months old and the caravan is about a kilometre away! What if he needs a feed?!"

She spits back, "You have NO *idea* how much we respect you."

"Well, you AREN'T SHOWING IT!" I yell at her.

I hurriedly get my four year old sorted, bundle all my stuff into the pram and high-tail it to the caravan with my nervous daughter in tow. I am absolutely *fuming*.

I storm over to the caravan and my father-in-law is sitting outside the caravan with my baby boy wrapped in another blanket (they even have to use their own stuff with my babies; I feel *so* raped right now). He notices my face as I quickly walk up.

"Why didn't you tell me you were going?" I demand and reach out for my baby, taking him into their caravan to change his nappy on their bed.

He is defensive and his tone of voice says "let's fight".

"He was cold. I just thought I would bring him here and wrap him in a blanket."

I shake my head at him, showing him *exactly* how I am feeling about him and this situation.

My daughter is hovering near me and I am almost shaking with rage.

Triggered by the last four years of boundary crossing, I am *OVER* their disrespectful ways of just "doing as they please" with my children as if I am merely the incubator.

"Why didn't you tell me though?! I was literally a metre away in the change rooms; all you had to do is to knock on the door."

I finish changing the nappy. I realise my mother-in-law is in the van and she is on the phone.

I take no notice of her.

I face off with my father-in-law, daughter at my leg and my baby boy in my arms.

"Stop disrespecting me!" I demand to his face.

He slams his hand on the kitchen table.

"Don't you *dare* say I disrespect you!" He is old fashioned, offended that a woman is facing-off with him.

It's not the first time he's indicated he is a misogynist.

I slam my own hand on his kitchen table.

"You *DO* disrespect me!"

I then move out of the van and leave them with daughter in tow, baby in my arms, and also pushing the pram with a spare hand which I manage to produce from fucking nowhere. The extra hands you grow as a mother is simply incredible.

As I get to about two-hundred metres away, my mother-in-law pathetically dribbles, "Oh well, goodbye then."

I sigh, "Come on then, walk us to the car if you're going to be respectful."

We get to the car. I buckle children in and put the pram in the boot.

I am beyond reasoning with and I cannot believe what has just happened.

I say goodbye to this woman that I no longer have any shred of respect for.

These people are complete assholes, and I will not try for them again I decide then and there.

Once I am driving away I ask Emily if she is okay. She nods, "Yes, but why is Poppy so angry?"

I tell her it's because he did the wrong thing by taking away the baby without asking and mummy had to yell at him.

She nods.

I am even angrier and I ring Frank.

He answers straight away and I launch into what has just happened.

"Yeah, I know. I heard most of it." he admits instantly.

I am shocked, "What do you mean?"

"I was on the phone to Mum when you and Dad were bluing."

I then realise that his Mum *was* on the phone whilst in the van. *Oh God*, I think. *What a pain in the arse she is! She just cannot help herself and HAS to ring her little boy.*

"Yeah right, so you are going to sort this out then, aren't you?"

I demand solutions FAST and tell him, "I'm so done, SO, SO DONE with all this boundary crossing *BULLSHIT*."

My wild-woman DEMANDS retribution and I tell him he is to ring his father and I will accept no less than an apology to me *and* Emily, as she is upset at witnessing her grandfather go off at her mother.

He reassures me that this will happen.

However, it doesn't.

It is explained to me over time, that because his father is old fashioned, as is his mother, they find it incomprehensible that a young lady would *dare* speak back to an older male.

This is starting to really wear me down.

The angst from this again spills over into our marriage: We are arranging for my son's baptism a month later and anything to do with a party for us creates tension.

Frank doesn't deal well with stress and I am left to arrange everything, which, on top of feeding a new baby all night long, means I am on edge and very, *very* fucking tired.

But I keep showing up and doing ALL the things, every moment of the days and the nights, for my baby, for my daughter and for myself.

I try my best to be everything to my husband, but I am so tired and worn-out emotionally from his family, I find it hard to touch him.

So in the lead-up to the eve of the baptism, after a few drinks, even his frustration and carnal anger at me rears its head.

We are sitting in the lounge room and I have been enjoying a few wines with my best friend and soon-to-be Godmother to my son.

He comes home a little late and I realise he is a little drunk.

He grabs a drink and plonks himself beside me.

We are all chatting away about the next day, about friends and family, and then he says something about my vagina.

My friend and I stop and look at him: It's really awkward and not quite what we ever expect from him. *Woah, he must be PISSED AS*, I think to myself, quite shocked as normally this is what *I* would be saying when drunk, not him.

I tell him not to be silly and as I say, "Don't say that," I tap him lightly on his leg with the back of my left hand.

BAM! He punches me in the left leg.

"OW!" I recoil, mortified that he did that. I am doubly mortified that he has done it in front of my friend.

"What?" he says, a sneer on his face and a glint of hatred in his eye.

"That didn't hurt – I only hit you *this* hard," and with that, BAM! – he punches me in the left arm.

I recoil again and this time stand up to get away from him.

"Ow, you CAN'T do that!" I keep saying. "You just cannot do that!"

My best friend gets up and states she needs to go to bed.

He appeals to her and tries to get her on his side by saying, "You saw it didn't you? It didn't hurt."

My friend pauses, then she says this: "All I know is that if Elizabeth is saying it hurts, then it must hurt. That's all I know. Goodnight."

I go out of the room with her and say goodnight to her, rubbing my arm and leg and then I check on my babies. Both are asleep.

I go back to the lounge room and slide the door shut for privacy.

"What on earth are you doing?! You can't hit me; after everything we've gone through you are *NOT* allowed to hit me."

He is lying on the couch, appearing relaxed and calm, and he pauses before saying to me, "You are a fucking cunt of a thing. I hate you. You fucking bitch."

I am shocked.

It freezes me harder than the punch.

The absolute hatred in the tone of his voice, the absolute complete and utter disgust, makes me stop. It's not actually what he has said, but *how* he has said it. The hatred is vicious.

I say nothing in response.

I stand up and walk out of the room and I sleep on the floor of the children's bedroom that night.

"Well," I say to myself, "we're over then."

But we weren't.

I was three more years away from having the courage to say the words: "I want a divorce."

The rest of that year was horrible.

I was verbally abused three more times, and each time I would leave him for a week to try to 'force the hand of change'. It was a move a psychologist was trying to help me use: try to force him to change. I honestly wished to have my husband back.

I truly wished that it would somehow all work out again and that I would be in love with him and that he would love me back.

But it just didn't or couldn't happen. We had moved into our separate lanes and there we stayed.

In the October of that year, after having left him three times due to the verbal abuse, things were kind of rocky but I had goals to attain and I was back studying to become a Lactation Consultant.

This time I needed to fly back to another state to sit an exam and with that distance I decided I just couldn't leave my son.

I was convinced to leave my daughter with Frank, which I bemoaned, however I realised a study trip with a nearly five year old and nearly one year old solo might be a stretch, even for me.

So I arranged for a babysitter to help me out during the study sessions and exams. She was a student nurse that I had never met, but she was advertised on the student web page and we chatted online for a bit. She sounded perfect: Qualified in first aid, used to babysit as a teenager, and happy to help a fellow nursing student.

I hated leaving my children (I still do) and I was very anxious about leaving my daughter.

I knew that she would probably be left with the in-laws with their intrusive ways; it honestly felt like they were molesting me when they devoured my children.

It felt like they had put their hands up my vagina and taken my babies out themselves.

They had such "ownership" of my children when they were around me, that it made me feel sick to my stomach.

Intrusive and boundaryless, they wouldn't know how to spell 'respect', let alone give it.

So with that chip on my shoulder, I boarded my plane and flew to another city, another state and another level of stress that changed my life.

Once I landed and got to uni (I had caught the early morning flight so that I would have as little time away from my daughter as possible: *Only one night away from her, I can do this!* I was saying positively to myself), I quickly rang the babysitter and she hurried to meet me.

I literally met her for all of a minute, she grabs the pram and I ask her to just stay on campus please.

She agrees and I ran up to the classroom to begin the exam preparation.

After ten minutes, I realise that I hadn't asked her to show me ID. I try to flick it away as being silly, but the fears rise up within me and I think, *Shit! What if she kidnapped him just then and she wasn't actually the babysitter?*

I message her on Messenger to come up to the room and just show her ID through the windows in the door.

My phone pings: The notification says that the user is no longer connected.

I stare at my phone. *What the fuck?*

I message her again, "Can you please just hold your ID up to the window of the classroom?"

I stare at my phone; the message doesn't go through and I instantly feel the rush of absolute panic.

I look up at the teacher and excuse myself to go to the bathroom.

I press the buttons on the lift as quickly as possible and, like in a movie, I was frantic.

She can't have gone far, I'm thinking to myself. *I just left her.*

I get out of the lift and run to where I had just met the babysitter.

There is no one around.

My heart sinks and I start to run: I am calling out for my son and calling out her name.

I rush through all the facilities; it's a small campus and being a weekend, it is deserted.

So why can't I find her?!

My panic becomes extreme.

I get to the last part of the uni, the only part she could be as I'm sure I've checked all areas, and as I stare out the back gate – the *locked* back gate, my body shuts down and my mind says, *Fuck! My son has just been kidnapped*.

I have images of myself running through the city screaming his name, and I am absolutely terrified.

"FUCK!"

(My heart is racing even as I write this, and any mother that has lost their child in a shopping centre will resonate: That moment you think they are gone is like death but you're still bloody breathing.)

I start to run. I run to the security office and there is no one there.

He was just there a minute ago! I think frantically.

I dial the phone that is outside the office and he answers.

"Hello?" I am panicky and very fucking terrified.

"Yes, Security. What's the matter?"

I tell him I am looking for a lady with a pram. He says, "The lady with the blonde hair?"

I reply, "No, no, that's me. I'm looking for the babysitter."

It should be noted that during all of this frantic panic, I am still ringing this babysitter every second. I am messaging her, ringing her phone and constantly checking the messaging services.

I am *beside* myself.

He says, "Why? Don't you know her?"

I freeze again. It sounded like he said, "Why did you hand your baby over to someone you don't even know?"

I freak out. I ask him if there's anywhere else on campus that she might be.

He is now in front of me, after having walked back from his detour around campus.

"There's the library," he points out.

It's right near where I had dropped off my son and when the security guard opens the door, I see them.

The babysitter is logging onto a computer and my son is sitting happily in his pram.

I run over to them and collapse beside the pram onto the floor.

I am crying, breathing heavily and my body cannot move.

The security guard asks if that's all.

I nod and mumble, "Yes, thank you," and the babysitter is sitting there apologising.

"I dropped my phone just before I met up with you and didn't realise it was broken. I saw you had messaged me but I couldn't log into my phone because the screen was cracked," she explained.

"I then turned my phone on and off to try to fix it, but when that didn't work I came into the library to log onto my messages via the computer. That's when you came in."

I am panting; I have one hand holding me up off the floor and the other is holding my son's leg.

I burst into tears of relief and frustration.

"I can't do this," I say, "I just can't do this."

The babysitter kneels down beside me. "I'm so sorry," she keeps saying, "I didn't mean to scare you."

"No, no, it's okay," I reassure her as I am slowly gathering my wits together.

"But I cannot do this; I have to quit this subject and go home."

I tell her I'm going to go upstairs and quit. She says she will wait to see what I decide to do and that I can just message her as she will log onto her messages on the computer and be in touch.

I hold my son in my arms, pressing my face into his body and just breathe into him.

I keep thinking, *I can't believe I nearly lost you*, and I am slowly gaining strength with every breath and with every cuddle.

I get up to the classroom and ask if I can speak to the teacher alone.

She comes out and I tell her what has just transpired. I tell her I cannot do this anymore and that I need to quit.

She gets the subject head to come and talk with me to discuss this.

The subject head introduces herself and my heart sinks.

In the lead up to this trip, I have been emailing her and I found her to be rude. I myself can come across as rude too, when I am being upfront.

I was asking for support to bring my son into the classroom. She was saying it wasn't appropriate and was offering no solution for me to do this. I had accused her of not being supportive of parents who are studying, thus the anxiety of now meeting her face-to-face.

I had been a tad rude to her and now I needed her help.

"Oh, you're Elizabeth," she says.

I apologise immediately: "I'm so sorry about the emails, I'm so sorry about everything, but I just cannot do this. I thought that I had lost my son." And with that, I burst into tears again.

I am sobbing into my boy's stomach, my shoulders moving up and down with fear and grief.

It has overwhelmed me, all of this: the eleven years in leading up to this moment, the continued stressors at home; I miss my daughter, fear my husband and nearly lost my son.

Plus I am trying to complete a university degree at the same time.

Something has to give and for me, it's my nerves. It's always my bloody nerves.

I cannot stop crying. The subject head softens and places her hand on my shoulder. "Come in here and we will talk." She gently guides me to a lecture hall that is adjacent to the classroom I am in and we sit down.

I start to calm down; she gets the tissues and we start to talk.

I explain everything. She starts to understand the context of my stressed emails to her and this time, she tries to help me.

"Okay," she says. "You're all the way over here now. I'm sure flights aren't cheap and I just think... Look, you're here now – why don't you try to make the best of the situation? Complete your studies sit the exam tomorrow and then fly home."

I listen. It feels hard to accomplish, but I really want to try as she does make a good point.

It was a fight-and-a-half to actually be allowed to spend the money on getting myself over here.

Demands of: "You'd better be paying me back by getting a good job and letting me retire soon," are thrown at me in the lead-up to me needing to make this study trip.

She then recommends that the babysitter, if it's okay with her, just take care of my son in this lecture theatre. It's not being used for the weekend and my classroom is right beside it.

I agree; my son will be just next door and I can drop in and see him whenever I like which appeals to the anxious mother within me who is very obviously expressing herself.

So I message the babysitter. She arrives, is spoken to by the head and it is agreed. She will look after him all day in this lecture theatre.

I part with him and strengthen my resolve to just do what I came here to do: pass this one subject.

It is a part of my second-year nursing degree. I actually used to want to be a nurse, but with my love of breastfeeding came a love for the organic and natural solutions. So the big push for pharmaceuticals has put me off the nursing career.

However, to become a Lactation Consultant, I need a certain amount of health subjects to be able to sit the ultimate in all exams for me: the International Board Certified Lactation Consultant exam.

I have done all the necessary research and the International Board requires me to complete this ONE subject before I can sit their exam.

I am getting it done and dusted before needing to spend another year studying lactation-specific subjects to prepare for the massive exam.

I also want to do my Diploma of Counselling at the same time, so I need to get this subject done *now* so that I am free for the next two years in preparation for the huge exam.

I get through the day, I pay the babysitter and we agree to meet the next morning on campus.

She is very kind and reassures me that he has been fine; I can see he is fine and I am grateful that the staff have tried to accommodate my situation.

I get back to my hotel room that night absolutely emotionally exhausted from the day's events.

My mind is fizzed after needing to jam more information into it, all whilst trying to breathe through the massive cortisol hit my body has taken that day.

My son seems nonplussed about the events and I am relieved we got through it. I do not take anything for granted right now with him and I cannot stop touching him.

I have had the fucking fright of my life.

I get changed, eat something and then jump on the phone to speak to my daughter.

I ring Frank.

He answers and it sounds echoey. I ask him where he is.

He tells me he has taken Emily out for dinner and I ask where and he tells me it's our favourite sporting bar. We had enjoyed chicken wings there when I was pregnant with our boy and so we reminisce kindly about that. It feels nice to have a familiar story between us and I lower my walls with him.

Getting away to study has caused a lot of tension between us: spending money usually did that with us.

I tell him about my day and he starts to get a bit upset with me.

Again, I am confused about his complete lack of empathy; it always makes me feel like I am in the wrong and starts to make me question myself. I don't realise at the time that I am being gaslit, and I take full responsibility for how I am making him feel.

I start to feel guilty. Perhaps he is right; I shouldn't have taken my son here, but the thought of being parted from *both* of my babies leaves me shivering. I tell him all is okay and I start to retract from the massiveness of the day and dull it down a lot so that I am not going to get in trouble for bringing my son with me.

I ask what he has done today and he tells me he mowed the lawn of our investment property in the same town that his parents live in.

It used to be our first home before we made the sea change and tried to escape our old lives: I from his parents; him from me.

I start to feel sick. "Where was Emily while you mowed the lawns?"

I know the answer and I feel sick about it. I am still reeling from the "stealing" of my baby boy whilst on holidays.

"I left her with Mum."

I go quiet.

The weight of my silence pisses him off and he is also still reeling from having to deal with his parent's moaning about his wife that 'crosses the line' with them. How dare she insist on having boundaries?

I take a deep breath and fail to control myself.

"Why did you have to mow the lawns?"

He then launches. "I knew you'd be upset with me. I knew it!"

We argue and then I stop: I still haven't spoken to my daughter yet and I realise that he said he was sitting in public...He is arguing with me, not just in front of my daughter, but in public!

"Can I speak with my daughter please?" I ask.

"No," he says bluntly.

"*What?*"

"No," he replies, "not with that tone of voice. I don't want you talking to my daughter with that tone of voice. You sound like a psycho."

I go cold, my heart freezes again and I fight.

"Frank, put her on the phone."

"No."

"Frank! *Please* put her on the phone!"

Clunk! He hangs up.

I look at my phone, stunned. *I cannot believe this!* I am FREAKING out. The cortisol rushes into my blood stream again and I press dial on my phone.

He hangs up on me.

I try this at least six more times until he eventually turns his phone off.

I gasp.

I look at my phone and my thoughts race. I rack my brain to see what I can do to get to my daughter.

I ring my best friend, the one from the country.

I am beside myself with anxiety. I am practically screaming down the phone that I cannot get a hold of my daughter, Frank has turned his phone off and has called me a psycho, and I nearly lost my son.

The whole day comes vomiting out and I am shaking. I am a mess, physically and mentally.

I collapse on the ground. I make sure my son is okay, and I start to cry.

"I don't know what to do!" I finish my phone call. She has no solutions for me and I cry whilst racking my brain: *What can I do?!*

I decide to change my flights. Fuck uni – I need to get home straight away!

I look up flights from this state to my own and the flight is at nearly midnight.

The cost, however, is hundreds of dollars that I do not have available to me right now.

I panic.

FUCK! I get up and pace the hotel room. My son is happily watching cartoons; I am pacing. I decide to have a shower and try to think. *My brain won't FUCKING WORK.*

I jump in the shower and turn on the water and press my head against the tiles.

"Fuck-fuck-fuck-fuck-fuck-fuck."

I am recharged by the change in my scenery and I get dressed, feel a little better and decide to ring our old friend the police officer.

He doesn't answer.

I leave a message.

He doesn't respond.

I ring my best friend.

We talk, much more calmly this time, and she tells me that I am too tired to fly; my financial resources mean that I need to just stay at the hotel and maybe I could try to catch an earlier flight home the next day.

I agree: I am absolutely exhausted. My babies are not good sleepers; I am very tired as my son is eleven months old, and I haven't slept more than two hours in a row this whole time, not to mention the fact that my marriage has been so stressful that my body is in extreme adrenal fatigue.

I go to sleep after trying Frank about a hundred times.

No connection. No daughter.

I cry myself to sleep cuddling my son.

Chapter 11

THE DARKNESS CONTINUES.

The next morning I am focused only on getting home. However, I first need to get out of sitting the exam at uni without failing my course, otherwise all of this would have been for nothing.

I actually don't care, I truly don't; I just want to get home to my daughter who I am feeling has been kidnapped from me. But there is something in me that doesn't want him to "win" by ruining my chances at having a career. So I still do the "right thing" and attempt to sort out my course before rushing off home.

I get dressed, pack and bundle my son into his pram, walking as fast as I can to the uni.

I am early and have to wait for everything to open up.

As I wait, the security guard from the day before starts his shift. He says 'hello' and I say 'hello' back. I am tense. Even seeing him makes me feel sick.

He nods and smiles at me and then goes into his office.

I get in the lift to where my exam is meant to be and I find a teacher straight away.

I explain what had occurred the evening prior: Not only am I stressed about having nearly lost my son, but I have now lost my daughter who has been kidnapped by her father. I am unable to get in contact with him and am trying every opportunity I can.

I explain I just cannot focus.

They are worried that I am wasting my trip; they focus on the uni aspect of this.

I get more insistent and ask them for the simple answer: If I do not sit this exam, will I fail the whole subject?

I am irritated they don't think of this. *Fuck wits*, I think to myself.

They seem to hustle together like hens, clucking about, saying this-and-that, and I want to shoo them away. They are annoying me in my anxiety.

The head chook agrees that, No, I will not fail my exam if I miss it.

Obviously they are giving me a lot of leniency but they say they "understand my situation".

I reply to the babysitter who has asked if she is needed today: "No, thank you."

I hurriedly get into a taxi and get myself and my son to the airport.

I run straight to the desk to change my flights and am told that the only flight to my city is the flight that I am on.

I grit my teeth. *Of course it fucking is*, I think negatively.

I sit in the airport with my son, drinking coffee and breastfeeding him from time to time and just wait.

Hours pass by, and eventually I am able to board the flight. Nothing seems to go fast enough and in the midst of this storm that I am in, it all feels like slow motion.

I am so desperate to see my daughter that I cannot breathe.

I am in the zone of desperation: I cannot think about anything except my son in my arms, and seeing my daughter.

That's it.

I arrive in my city and it's when I try to find my car that I actually realise how deeply stressed I am.

I cannot find my bloody car!

I waste precious minutes (which feel like hours) walking up and down rows and rows of cars trying to find my car.

I can feel my legs shaking underneath me and I start to run. I need to get home: *Where the FUCK is this car?!*

I realise I am in the wrong section and thankfully I see it in the distance.

I am fuming by this stage, absolutely *fuming*. The stress is coming out in anger. *If I wasn't so stressed I would have found my car by now*, I think to myself.

I am angry at the kids' dad; angry at his fucking fucked-up ways.

I am wearing a necklace his mother gave me: I tear it off and throw it on the ground. I empty my handbag into my travel case and place it under the back tyre of the car.

Frank gave it to me for Christmas last year and I intend to run over it. *Fuck him!*

I am relieved to be on the road driving towards my baby girl.

Not quite a baby at four, but still, my baby girl.

I do not stop the entire drive home, nearly two hours, and I am an absolute bundle of nerves by the time I get there.

I pull up in the driveway. It is around six PM and I am absolutely *breaking* to see my daughter.

I take my son out of his car seat and notice my heart starts to race.

Fuck, I think. *Fuck!*

I don't want to see Frank…*What do I do?*

I tell myself: *It's make or break. Just keep your shit together, get your kids back and leave that fucking asshole in the morning.*

Survival mode kicks in and I calm myself down. This is to get my daughter back, I tell myself.

I open the front door and she is sitting on the couch on his lap. She runs up to me.

I am crouched on my knees, semi-collapsed to see her and give her the biggest cuddle. I squeeze her close to me. I hold back the tears, which actually aren't that close as I realise I am very, very fucking angry at her dad.

He says nothing.

He sits on the couch like a looming monster. The lights are all dimmed; it's like a horror movie.

I stand up and say nothing. He says nothing.

I look at him.

We stare at each other. I am in the hallway; he is still sitting in the semi-dark of the lounge room, and I'm not sure what he is thinking but I notice that I am definitely scared.

He says quietly and without emotion, "How was your trip?"

I answer robotically, "Good thanks."

That is it.

I play with my daughter for a bit and start to get both the kids ready for bed.

I put them to bed: I sleep with them, saying nothing more to him.

I lie in my daughter's bed with her, my son in the cot right next to it, and I start to plan my escape.

The next morning I get out of bed and am very thankful that Frank has already left for work.

I am so relieved. I can't stop playing with my daughter and am joyous to be with her again. I say nothing about the weekend she had with her "Daddy" and I turn on the TV for the kids, make a coffee and then start the day.

First thing to do is figure out how to get out of this relationship.

I have no idea what to do so I Google *"domestic violence help for women"* and put in the location of where I live.

The name of a government service pops up and I ring the number. There is an automated message: I have called them too early, however they provide an email address for me to begin my enquiry.

I email them telling them about what has just transpired and that there is a history of abuse.

I wait.

I bustle about with the kids, but check my phone and my computer whenever I can.

I receive an email not long after 9.30AM and I am asked if I am immediately safe and whether is it safe for me to speak on the phone.

I reply: "YES, please." and shortly after the phone rings.

The lady I speak to tells me what I need to do to talk to him about leaving without the kids being present.

I need to arrange to meet him at a café or public setting, place the kids with someone else and then ask him to leave.

I am scared, but determined.

"Okay," I say, "but what if he says 'sorry' and can change?"

"No," she replies with the most alarming, but truthful, statement I was yet to believe. "Leopards don't change their spots: He will never change."

She was right, of course. However, I always had hope.

I did what she said: I enlisted the help of a friend to have the kids that afternoon, texted Frank to meet up with me at a cafe that afternoon, and asked him to leave.

The conversation was the hardest thing I've ever had to do.

Sitting face-to-face with a man who had just justified kidnapping my daughter from me.

Justifying that everything he has *ever* said and done to me was my fault.

Justifying once again, that it was *my* fault he hung up on me and wasn't able to speak to my daughter for 48 hours.

I calmly asked him to go home, pack his things, and leave the house.

He demanded to know where the kids were and I just kept saying "safe" and "with a friend".

He was very angry, but the helpline was right: We were in a public setting so there was nothing he could really do.

He restrained himself because he liked to keep up the appearance that he was a good person. He stood up and left relatively calmly. I waited a few moments until I thought he had gone and I headed to my car too.

I peered nervously around the parking lot.

I was frightened that he would ambush me and hurt me, torture me to get the address of where the kids were and beat me up.

But he had gone. He had done what I asked, and so I drove back to my friend's house to debrief with her and decompress.

I waited with her for a few hours. We had dinner and talked and I wound down so that I could be of use to my kids and myself.

I thanked her for her support and drove home, sure that he would have left by then.

However, I drove past my house from the other direction just to make sure his car wasn't in the driveway.

It wasn't, so I headed home with the kids and we all went to bed in my bed, the kids tired from the day, me exhausted from exerting my muscle.

The rest of that week was wonderful. I had emails from the department head at uni saying they understood where I was coming from; in fact, she called me to speak about it all.

It was with great empathy that she allowed me to finish the subject with the work I had done and pass it based on my excellent results that I had produced for the prior eighteen months of study.

I was incredibly grateful: Finishing those subjects had been through sheer hard work and determination and a massive fight to have access to finances to follow my dreams.

Constantly told I was nothing because I didn't "earn money", Frank always made it known to me what a privilege it was for me to have things funded.

"You should be grateful I am supporting you with this."

"This better pay off. I'm working my guts out for you to sit at home and read books."

My kids and I were light-hearted and I felt like I was doing well.

I didn't miss him at all and yet there was a lack of strength within me still.

It worried me. I was tired.

I started to stumble at the thought of handing the children over to him.

I started to panic about missing out on spending time with my baby boy.

The thought of handing him over every second weekend became a monster in my mind, a dark spot in my heart, and I started to falter at the divorce thing.

I arranged for him to meet us at swimming on that Saturday, and when he walked in I had mixed emotions.

Oh shit, I thought. *I actually miss him.*

I admonished myself for feeling this way.

I realised then, how much I had been sickened by allowing his behaviour to become my normal.

I accepted his abuse so readily that seeing him after he had just done what seemed like the ultimate deal-breaker, meant that I was actually prepared to let this go.

Something within me recognised this and I felt sick about myself.

A deep loathing began to grow from within.

The realisation that I was okay with abuse and okay with his behaviour meant that I too was very, very sick.

I stared at him, noticed that he smelled amazing, and promptly burst into tears.

Mainly from the fact that I knew I wasn't going to honour myself, but also because I was aware, for the first time, how actually broken and sick I truly was.

I was in love with a man that abused me.

I was okay with being abused.

I made it okay and therefore I am as much to blame as he was.

He placed his hand on my knee and told me to pull it together.

I couldn't.

I buried my head into my arms, on full public display, and I sobbed loudly.

He put his arm around me and turned my face into his chest, mainly to hide that I was crying.

I knew that that was what he was really doing, but actually the fact that he was comforting me did what it always did to me. It gave me hope that he might actually love me and that everything would be alright.

"Why are you crying?" he says quietly into my hair.

"I miss you," I say into his chest. "I want you to come home."

I can feel his body relax, and then I feel it tense up again.

I know this energy, this feeling.

He is relieved I am behaving the way he wants. I have done what I always do: I have forgiven the behaviour.

But now I must pay for exerting my muscle.

No doubt he has stayed at his parents' for the week, and his embarrassment at having been "kicked out" of his own home is something I will pay for in some form of abuse.

I tense up, but the emotions being elicited by being held by someone are too strong for me to care.

My heart is soaring. I know the abuse is coming, but right now, in this moment, I have my husband back and I feel amazing.

I settle into his arms, into the moment, and watch the rest of my daughter's swimming lesson with red eyes and a flickering of hope in my chest.

The weeks and months afterwards are dark.

I am punished.

He firstly admonishes me for "kicking him out of his own home". This one I knew was coming, so I braced myself and allowed the words to sink in.

I take responsibility for it and apologise.

He is a man and that it is not good to kick a man out of his house he explains.

I say I am sorry.

We argue a little bit about the hanging up on me with my daughter, but I have made up my mind to stay with him, and so I let it go.

He is determined that he is right and he rams it home so hard that my nerves cannot handle the jarring of his incorrect justification.

I feel like it's better to shut up and just take it on the chin.

He also sleeps on the couch. For months.

At first he says he has just fallen asleep whilst watching TV.

The first night he comes home he does this and I carry a blanket out to him to cover him with it.

I recall looking at him with pity and love and fear all at once, not knowing exactly who he is and why I am in love with him still after all that he has done.

He has also stopped kissing me goodbye in the morning before work.

Even during the height of the abuse, when he would punch me, he would always kiss me on the forehead before going to work.

The morning kisses have stopped, and that is the thing I notice the most.

My inner-child starts freaking out at this.

I bring it up; he makes excuses.

I cry about it alone.

It destroys me internally more than all the other things he has ever done.

It is the moment, I believe, that I know that he has truly fallen out of love with me.

I decide that even though he doesn't love me, even though he is punishing me by sleeping on the couch (he admits this when I bring it up), I cannot leave my babies.

So I decide to create my "invisible jar".

I start drinking alcohol.

~

I'm sitting in my car. My son, who is now three-and-a-half years old, has been crying about not having his dummy for a while. I have actually pulled him out of playgroup early so as to escape the piercing eyes of the other mums who might see me not coping with his pain.

He feels pain because I am not giving him his dummy.

I have not weaned him off the dummy successfully. I have realised that I myself actually love using the dummy to soothe my babies and therefore, even when I said "No dummy", I kept on giving it back to him. This meant that he didn't have the habit broken and has learned that if he cries long enough I just cave.

I have been doing that a lot lately, but Frank has demanded that the dummy goes. If not for Frank, he would be getting that dummy back.

But today, I decided to not bring it. I try to distract him with playgroup and hope like hell that he forgets about it. Frank's insistence that the dummy is weaned off is loud and I am trying so hard to be a good wife as well as a good mother.

My son feels the tense energy coming from me so he wants his dummy even more.

He won't stop crying, so I pull over in my soccer-mum car and I begin the "freeze".

I just stare at the steering wheel. He cries and he cries and he cries.

I stare and I stare and I stare.

"I can't fucking move," I mumble to myself.

Wow, I think. *I can't even fucking think clearly enough not to mumble in my own mind.*

His cries get more insistent and I cannot handle it.

I cannot even look at him and my heart breaks again as I recall doing this to him.

I open the car door and get out. I stumble around to the back of the car with my phone in one hand and I find a puddle behind the car. *What I am looking for? I don't know...a hole, maybe?*

It is a dried out puddle and I sit in it. A semi-hole.

I am semi-everything right now: semi-mum, semi-woman, semi-alive.

I can hear my son from the car door that is open and I stare at the dirt in the bottom of the puddle and I feel nothing.

I just stare and stare and stare at that dirt.

I am not sure how long I am there for before a man drives in and stops near me.

It must have been a sight: A soccer mum, sitting in a puddle at the rear of her car, driver door wide open, sounds of a crying child in the back seat... as if no one is going to stop.

"Are you ok?" he asks.

I manage to look up at him. I can't even speak.

I nod.

"Are you sure?" he insists.

"Um, yes," I manage to mumble. "Yes. I'm fine."

He doesn't believe me, I can tell, but he says, "Okay" and drives away slowly, watching me as I remain in the puddle at the back of the car.

I ring Frank.

He answers abruptly.

Things are not great, not great *at all*.

"Yes?"

"Um...." I falter.

I fail. I stumble; I can barely speak.

"I can't get up," I try to explain.

"What the fuck do you mean?" He is angry and tired of the emotions. He is not happy with me: He is just not happy and I really need someone and he is all I have.

But he hates me. I feel it in every syllable that comes out of his mouth.

"I'm sitting in a puddle, Frank, at the back of the car. He won't stop crying because I forgot his fucking dummy. That's what's up." I am angry; I speak angrily. I am always angry.

All I want is for him to love me back and he doesn't so it makes me angry.

"What fucking dummy? I thought you'd stopped giving it to him. See, this is why he's crying: You can't stick to things. Here's what you do: get the fuck up out of the puddle, get back in the car and go get his dummy then. I can't believe you're calling me with this shit. I hate to be the one to say this, but you need to stop this shit."

I freeze. *Wow*, I think, t*hat's marriage for you*, and my self-esteem plummets even further. I have no idea how much further down it can go. But it is definitely leaving me at a rate faster than I can breathe.

I put the phone down on the ground, push myself up out of the dirt and get back into the car.

I have hung up on Frank, I think. I don't know or care anymore.

I look back at my son and he is straining against his seatbelt, his tears absolutely streaming down his face, and my heart stops and breaks into a thousand pieces.

I instantly snap out of the freeze. I hurriedly grab him out of his car seat and cuddle him in my lap for the longest time.

"I love you so much. I love you, I love you, I love you," I murmur into his hair for the entire time, my heart breaking again and again that I made him cry.

I then start to cry, and cry, and cry.

I am mortified. I am so broken. I am fucking broken *again*. *FUCK*.

But I know deeply that I needed to break today because it's all got to end. This insanely hateful marriage and the life that I am living with Frank is horrible.

Having your partner hate you is a disturbing feeling. Hating your partner back is even worse.

I have never felt so alone in all my life.

As I cuddle my son and grieve the fifteen years I have been with Frank, I think back to the first time I realised my husband didn't respect me. *Why didn't I stop it then?* but I quickly stop myself thinking those thoughts and remind myself that two children is the reason I don't regret those years.

But, wow, how much I didn't see... How much love clouded my vision.

Love truly is blind, I think to myself. In fact, it's debilitatingly so.

It is not because I am weaning my son off his dummy that I am tense, nor is it the state of the marriage: It's the anxiety about what had happened to Emily earlier that year.

A few months ago, we learned that she had been molested that January by Frank's older brother's son, Emily's cousin, who was seven years older than her. It's disgusting. I absolutely lost my shit and spent days and weeks beating myself up for letting her go stay at her stupid grandparents' house.

I blame myself *entirely* for what happened to her and I spend every waking minute comforting her and trying to find support for her.

I, too, was molested by a family member at around that age. The perpetrator, my stepbrother, was five years older than me; I was eight at the time. I recall it nearly killed me in my twenties. The difference here is that I am a mother who is supportive of her daughter and that we have found out about the incident.

Thank GOD I know about it: *Imagine if we didn't know and kept sending her to those fucking assholes.*

Her grandmother, upon learning about this (*I mean, she was meant to be watching her!*) says: "Oh well, we were all molested back in our day and we turned out fine."

Yes - pick your jaw up off the ground - that was her reaction.

I am sickened. The level of sickness this family had was so deep I realised it was never-ending.

Frank demanded to have Emily get back to together with the cousin and "make friends" as they are a "close family" and that is "important to him".

I almost vomited in my mouth when he said all of this and I fought back.

"Absolutely NOT," I say to him and spend all my time finding evidence to ensure that my gut instincts are right. There is *NO WAY* she is going to see that little prick ever again, I think to myself.

The lack of support for Emily made me sick. I couldn't believe that Frank wouldn't go to the police with me to protect her and he argued with me that "This is my brother" whilst I angrily spat back, "This is our daughter!"

I knew that I was well and truly done. I had NO respect left for him and if I didn't go, my children would eventually disrespect *me*.

I had to leave.

The words "I want a divorce" took me over seven years to say.

They were always on the back of my mind, always needed to be said, but I was too scared.

I was scared that I would regret saying them, scared that I would change my mind.

But once I said them, I felt free – freer than I had ever been in my entire life.

Yet this led to the soul-jarring experience of needing to co-parent with someone that I had left due to abuse, someone that my soul was screaming at me to get away from.

It started fine.

It was awkward and I was getting messages regularly asking me to change my mind, to make it work. I constantly had to explain to Frank that there was no going back, reminding him of the abuse and was repeatedly told that he didn't know what I was talking about. But then it fast-tracked into me needing to remove the children from him for three months a year later: He had "scared them" by having his best friend abuse me in front of them, resulting in two Intervention Orders and two very scared children that didn't want to see their father.

Frank did what he was told to get them back: counseling – and the kids eventually came around to him. At the time of my writing this book, the children are older and still see him. They "see his shitness" and say things like, "You know what he's like" and "I'd only tell you this Mum, I can't talk to Dad about this stuff", but they love him anyway. Regardless of how shit your dad is, you don't realise it until you're an adult and you love them, shitty ways and everything.

They know that I am the stable one, I am the one to be there for them and that I am the listener. Want to fall apart? Mummy is here.

As of right now, I am getting another Intervention Order on him as he cannot help but continue to call me and abuse me, mainly trying to control me, and I now give him absolutely nothing.

It is a shame he couldn't grow up and be amicable, but I know that he thinks he is actually being nice. Even after a threatening phone call to me he would swear to your face that he spoke nicely to me. Narcissist.

So although I become "free" from the marriage, there is much to repair.

My soul had finally spoken up, but she was very, very faint.

My spirit felt like shreds of paper, torn into a million pieces.

I needed to put her back together again.

So I started searching for Elizabeth.

It became my obsession to ensure that I searched for every single last shred of torn paper, and then put it all back together with superglue. I was going to rise so high from the ashes of my shattered self that no one would be able to miss me, most especially my beautiful children.

Chapter 12

WHAT HAPPENS WHEN WE BECOME PARENTS?

When a mother gets pregnant, her brain shrinks by five percent. That is, they have actually measured that the mass of grey matter in a mother's brain shrinks by five percent. This is nature's way of making sure she gets "tunnel-vision" about what is now the most important thing: preparing for, and taking care of, her baby.

This grey matter takes years to re-form and it's actually a necessary part of nature to ensure that a mother is completely focused on just taking care of her baby.

A human baby is the most defenceless of all creatures in the world. Unlike a lot of mammals that are on their feet and walking within minutes of being born, a human baby only has their senses to stay alive.

That is why if a baby is left in a cot or on a playmat by itself, it will wave its arms around and cry. The waving of arms is to move the grass and therefore alert the attention of the caregiver. Our DNA doesn't know we are born into modern society: our natural instincts are those of survival. We only have our five senses when we are born with which to stay alive.

So I tell you truly, with deep reassurance, that a baby who is wakeful and insists on being "on" mum or dad is a survivor.

This baby knows he needs to feel, and touch the caregiver: It's intrinsically a matter of life or death.

A man, during and post-birth, also has his "brain changes".

A man will start to develop new neuronal pathways in his brain throughout the pregnancy but mainly once he sees his baby.

Think about it from a cave man perspective: The new neurons will help a man to think with more spatial awareness, giving him the capacity to hunt further, see further, to protect his new family.

He needs these new pathways to develop more empathy in his brain as he now has two people to take care of.

In modern-day society, the development of these new pathways in a man's brain can feel either overwhelming or empowering for him.

The man who has done "work on himself", or is at least ready to, will find this empowering.

These are the times to create more, do more and make more decisions.

You have a bigger brain right now, so enjoy this and get to work on creating a bigger and better life!

As for the man that is ill, narcissistic and broken (whether he knows it or not), he will collapse with this new responsibility. He will either leave his new family, collapse and turn to drugs/drinking/cheating, or turn back to his family of origin who are probably the reason he is a collapsed man too. He is unable to rise into his new role as a father and therefore collapses,

making life harder for the mother. Of course, he misses out on the empowerment readily available to him because he simply cannot accept himself.

The modernisation of society has collapsed a lot of men.

They don't need to be the hunters and gatherers anymore.

How many men that you know of could rise to this responsibility?

How have they been raised?

Do you think it's too late for a collapsed man?

Well, of course not: A human being is as ready for change as they say they are.

I myself have undergone incredible transformations all because I have been willing to say I will change. I have had many years of my life whereby I was unable to "see myself" truthfully, but then one day I decided the pain of letting life step all over me was over.

I needed to start to listen. Stop talking and listen.

My role as a mother helped to kickstart my transformation but, to be fair to myself, it did start years prior.

It is also possible for a mother to collapse.

In our society where drug problems are a reality, and I myself took many drugs prior to becoming a mother, it is common for a mother to collapse and escape her responsibilities by turning back to drugs, or alcohol, or her family of origin.

So, do you realise if you are with a collapsed husband or partner? What if you are collapsed?

What can you do?

In Book one: Rise of the Mother I talk about how to prepare yourself as a parent.

The meditations are available at https://www.patreon.com/riseofthemother

It is never too late to change your life and "rise" as a parent.

The future of our world depends on you "having your shit together" so that you can raise happy, healthy and emotionally secure children. Children that will always have the capacity to rise themselves, because you made darn sure they could – by doing it yourself first.

Chapter 13
MOVE FORWARD - ALWAYS MOVE FORWARD

"I am relentlessly devoted to evolving.

Every tear I have shed will not be in vain.

Every heartache I have felt will not go unhealed.

Every cry from my soul will never again be pushed down and silenced in an attempt to please someone else who doesn't see me, doesn't feel me or doesn't hear me.

I am claiming my rise as a woman each and every day.

With each present moment I am focused on opening my heart to everything life has to offer me.

Whatever the Divine/God needs me to do, be or feel.

Wherever I am needed to be in service the most.

And with my babies, I am a mother who is untouchable."

xxx

I am okay now. I have a lovely life with my two children. They are growing up and the days of trauma are slowly fading into the past.

For the children, it fades faster than for me: Children are resilient. However, I too, had childhood trauma and it reared its ugly head when I became an adult. So I don't bury my head in the sand with the kids. I don't assume that just because they mostly have smiles on their faces that they are okay.

I know that the things they've seen, especially with their father, will scar them.

So I wake up every day and I work with the children, and especially on MYSELF, to mend those scars that no one can see in us. I am passionate about ensuring that we become completely healed, with no residue from the battles we have fought. Especially me.

In saying that, one of the main things we have to learn is that it is okay to not be okay.

However I truly believe that there is absolutely NO EXCUSE for a human being in this day and age to say that they have no idea how to become a better person.

As a parent it is *essential* that you pay attention to how you are behaving in front of your children – especially if you are the primary care-giver.

If you have anger issues, sort them out by seeing a counsellor.

If you have weight issues, enlist the help of a personal trainer and dietician. If you have issues with anxiety, start meditating or see a psychologist.

The tools that are available are so numerous that it is actually *EXCITING* to be able to try them all to see how high you can rise!

Other methods to rise are as follows:

Reading books, enlisting the help of a counsellor, joining a women's or men's circle, do group therapy, attend a Church or club, meet like-minded parents, attend a parenting workshop, go on a health retreat, find a psychologist, change up your nutrition to nourish your body (a nourished body equals a nourished mind), start exercising, explore the Internet for solutions to your "problems", watch documentaries that will compliment your transitions, find out who you are and never *NEVER* stop.

Never ever give up. Your children deserve that.

The ONLY thing you need to be doing as a parent is working on becoming the best version of yourself.

Then when you get to that place of "being better" that you were aiming for, keep striving to be better than that! Keep going!

The better you are, the better your children are going to be.

You have the choice and there is no better *'why?'* than your children.

I wish you well on your endeavours, and pray that I have inspired you to NEVER EVER stop rising to be the best parent you can possibly be.

xxx

RESOURCES FOR HELP

I get it: you are scared.

Fear runs your life when you are in a relationship of abuse. You continue to accept abuse until it feels normal. But it is not normal and there is help out there.

Here are some resources for you to reclaim your life.

https://www.acf.hhs.gov/fysb/programs/family-violence-prevention-services/programs/ndvh

https://ncadv.org/get-help

https://www.thehotline.org/

https://www.mayoclinic.org/healthy-lifestyle/adult-health/in-depth/domestic-violence/art-20048397

https://www.respect.gov.au/?gclid=Cj0KCQjwtvqVBhCVARIsAFUxcRsWkooPRZ-42RJ5aI3ieOdhLoybKZBvGpwYajKPNuHb0X8QhGcCnJcaAgm1EALw_wcB&gclsrc=aw.ds

https://www.1800respect.org.au/

https://www.dss.gov.au/our-responsibilities/women/programs-services/reducing-violence/help-and-support

https://orangedoor.vic.gov.au/

https://www.safvcentre.org.au/

If you cannot find a counsellor or IBCLC to help you on your journey, you can book a consult with me here:

riseofthemother@gmail.com

If you are interested in running your own business so you can stay at home with your baby, then contact me here:

riseofthemother@gmail.com

Find me on Instagram:

https://www.instagram.com/savingtheworldoneboobatatime/

About the Author

Shona Reidy lives in Victoria, Australia and is a mother to two beautiful children. She enjoys breath work, meditation, bike rides and long walks on the beach. For Shona, life is busy as a single parent and nothing has ever beaten the feeling she has when witnessing her children grow and walk their own paths as strong and creative human beings. Her daughter was the beginning of her incredible journey, and her son is the perfect completion of her experience in motherhood.

Through journeying extensively herself, Shona has dedicated the last twelve years to helping other mothers rise and walk their own journeys to become the best mothers they can be. Her hope is that the role of mother becomes a more valued one in society, and is recognized monetarily so that mothers don›t have to "leave" their babies to earn money.

www.ingramcontent.com/pod-product-compliance
Lightning Source LLC
Chambersburg PA
CBHW061943070426
42450CB00007BA/1040